How we view Christmas is often directly connected to how we view the Savior and the Gospel message. As someone that loves and sometimes over-sentimentalizes Christmas, I found myself very refreshed and challenged to think more deeply. This book is bold, wise, and fun—and I'm confident it will increase your love for Christmas, and your love for Jesus every day of the year.

Kevin Palau

President of the Luis Palau Association

'Christmas is not sentimental, it is instrumental.' Josh Moody helps us see that Christmas doesn't need to be only a time of hurried traditions and exhausting activity, it can be a season God uses to change our lives. This book will help you thoughtfully celebrate the true magic of Christmas: God making peace with us through the incarnation of Christ.

Heather Win Lefebvre

Author of *The History of Christmas: 2,000 years of Faith, Fable and Festivity*

The birth of Jesus Christ radically changed the course of human history. Yet multitudes of people, both within and without the church, have a view of Christmas marked more by sentimentality than by the Scriptures. *How Christmas Can Change Your Life* provides a trustworthy guide to understanding the real meaning of Christmas.

Al Jackson

Pastor, Lakeview Baptist Church, Auburn, Alabama

D0318483

JOSH MOODY

How Christmas Can Change Your Life

ANSWERS TO THE TEN MOST COMMON
QUESTIONS ABOUT CHRISTMAS

CHRISTIAN
FOCUS

paperback ISBN 978-1-5271-0408-2
epub ISBN 978-1-5271-0457-0
mobi ISBN 978-1-5271-0458-7

Published in 2019
by
Christian Focus Publications Ltd,
Geanies House, Fearn, Ross-shire
IV20 1TW, Scotland, UK
www.christianfocus.com

A CIP catalogue record for this book is available from the British Library.

Designed by
Pete Barnsley (Creativehoot.com)

Printed by Bell & Bain, Glasgow

Contents

Introduction

It's that time of year again. Sleigh bells. Christmas carols. The winter 'holidays', or, as Christians call it, 'Christmas.' What's all the fuss about? How can I make the most of Christmas this year if I am Christian? And why should I think about Christmas—and not just the winter 'holidays'—if I'm not a Christian?

This little book is designed to help you answer those questions in practical, as well as in intellectually satisfying, ways. It can't get to every question you might have: the book is too short to attempt to have a rigorous theology of the incarnation (for instance). But it can do what it is designed to do: be a good give-away to friends and colleagues, and a stimulus to fresh inspiration to live for Christ this Christmas.

As you start to read the book, let me give you some initial pointers or words of direction. You can start from the beginning if you want, but you don't have to. You can dive in pretty much anywhere to any of the questions and find it helpful. Also, why not pray before you read the book? Ask God to help you find the real meaning of Christmas this year. Another idea is to take this book and use it to do a series of studies about the real meaning of Christmas in your small group. They can be a good starting point for conversation. You might (preachers alert!) even like to use it as the basis for a sermon series. If you want to use it as the basis for a sermon or Sunday School series, then pick four of the questions that seem particularly meaningful to the people you are speaking to, and use those as the basis for a study. You'll obviously still have to do your own work for that teaching as this book is (again, by design) brief and to the point. If brevity is the soul of wit, it is certainly in the spirit of Christmas not to load you down with too much heavy theology.

So, dismiss the ghost of Christmas past (good or bad) and welcome the real meaning of Christmas: Christ is born this day, King, Lord, Immanuel, the Savior!

Xmas texes me
tells me
teaches me

Can Christmas Help Me With My Problems?

As a pastor the most common question I am asked about Christmas has nothing to do with Christmas as such. It has to do with the feeling that people have at Christmas that everyone else's life is perfect, and they are more aware that there is some difficulty in their own life. When they look around at the TV programs—*It's a Wonderful Life, A Christmas Story*, etc.— they seem to be presented with a view of life where everyone is doing just fine. And Christmas then has a bittersweet feeling: sweet because of all the festive spirit; bitter because they do not feel very festive on account of their own difficulties or problems.

The answer to this is that actually in Christmas there is help. Christmas is not a message about how everyone has perfect lives, and how we need to attain the same level of material success, or emotional happiness, or 'live the dream.' Christmas is a message about how all of us can find help from Jesus to overcome our problems and live in a way that pleases God, honors Him, and is ultimately and eternally satisfying.

The message of the angels at the first Christmas was, 'Glory to God in the highest, and on earth peace among those with whom he is pleased!' It was not, 'Look at all those other people with their cool lights, parties, fun, family, and feel really bad about what you have by comparison.'

How can Christmas help me? We probably don't think of Christmas as 'helping' as such. Christmas is more something 'out there,' something that just happens to us—like a nice movie, or a sunset that we can watch with a smile on our face. But Christmas can really change our lives. And in this first chapter we are seeing how it can really help us, make a difference, set our lives on a new trajectory. There are many ways that it can do this, but in this chapter I just want to suggest four. Can you think of others? Here are those four ways:

1. Christmas takes me out of me

The biggest problem most of us have is that we think too much about ourselves. Of course, there is nothing wrong—and much right—about considering how we can gain a good esteem of who we are in Christ. The problem with the so-called 'self-esteem' movement is not its laudable goal (to ensure that people feel good about themselves) but its ineffective method. If I look at myself too carefully it is very unlikely I will feel good about myself. I am liable to end up with a strange kind of self-deceit, whereby in order to gain more self-esteem I lose much genuine authenticity. The truth is that there is much that is not esteem-able about each of us. We are, as the Bible tells us, and as our consciences confirm, sinners, unable to live up to our own standards, let alone God's standards. We need something more than mere assertion, against the evidence, that we really are very very special people. What we need is solid ground, a firm foundation, upon which we can design the architecture of our lives.

And here is where Christmas, indeed the Christian story as a whole, helps so much. The greatest story there ever was is not about me at all. It is not about you either. It is about *Him*. This is actually a profound help. The story of my life is not my story; it is His story. Think of how satisfied, completed, joyful you are when you are lost in admiration of a beautiful sunset, or painting, or listening to your favorite music. Like that, but much more, Christmas helps us by encouraging us to worship, to lose our self-focus, and be lost in sheer wonder at the scale of the universe, the humility of God, the sacrifice of Jesus. It is such a relief to be immersed in a story whose hero is not me. Where the main character is not a foil for really marketing something to us that makes us feel that we are the center of the universe. Where the thrust of the narrative is to take us out of ourselves, to transcend our failings and faults, by being soaked in gospel grace in this story. Think on Christmas. Reflect on it. Spend time in the narrative and the story together: an advent calendar, a set of Christmas Bible readings, church attendance, conversation with friends, family traditions. All these and more can release us from what C. S. Lewis called our 'solitary conceit.' The greatest story that was ever told gives us relief from navel gazing by inspiring us to think about, and rejoice in, something else—Someone Else—other than me.

2. Christmas tells me my life has meaning

If one young pregnant girl, out of wedlock, can play such a significant role in the salvation of the world, how can I really think that my life is too small to be important? Mary's role is never to be repeated. But the pattern that God here identified is ongoing: He loves to use the weak things of this world, the things that are not; in our weakness His power is made perfect. His grace is sufficient. How encouraging is this! Look at Mary's vulnerability. Look at her lack of power and status. Look at her observing all the ways that people around her would easily have sneered at her. Can you hear the accusations from the relatives, or so-called friends, who thought that her pregnancy was a sign of her sexual sin? She was just one young woman. There was nothing (apparently) special about her. In a culture that prized the masculine, and the status of hierarchy and institutional authority, God chose to pick a young woman—with nothing to commend herself to anyone else, with no great resources or residual inherited authority— and use her to bring about the salvation of the world. This is how God worked through Mary. It is how God worked through the apostle Paul in his weaknesses. It is how God delights to work, ultimately through the apparent foolishness of the cross of Jesus Christ. How encouraging is this! Your life, whether famous or not, is not thereby defined as meaningless. All God requires is faith and faithfulness. Look at Hebrews chapter 11! What distinguished all these individuals so mightily used by God was not their charismatic personalities, but their willingness to be used by God, and to trust Him despite the evidence around them or the accusations against them. Would you, Christian, therefore be encouraged: God can use you for great things! Remember the great phrase coined by D. L. Moody to inspire him in his commitment to Christ: 'the world has yet to see what God can do through one man fully committed to him.' Moody determined to be that man. Perhaps you do not feel that you are a clever person, a beautiful person, a fashionable person. But you can be *that* person, like Mary, a person committed to God! Christmas helps us to see the lie that significance has to do with bank balance, gender, size, strength, fame, beauty, wealth, large houses, or big new shiny cars. God used Mary, not a 'Queen Precious with perfect hair and mascara.' He can use me; He can use you. My life has significance. So does yours.

3. Christmas ~~persuades~~ teaches me that no problem is too big for God

We have heard that line before: no problem is too big for God. But it can seem so fake. Really? Is it really true that no problem is too big for God? What about *my* problems? What about the very real problems of the world around us? And anyway what does that *really* mean—no problem is too big for God—in practice? If we do admit that no problem is too big for God, are we then saying that, when faced with a problem, all we need to do is pray? That Christians should simply be passive in the face of adversity, and never stand up for themselves or counteract slander or accusations? It is easy to say from a pulpit that no problem is too big for God; it is much harder to believe it in the trenches of the First World War. Or out on the high seas when it's blowing a gale. Or when your marriage is falling apart. Or when you don't get the grades you need to go the college or university that you had set your heart on. It is not helpful to believe pious ideas if they cannot translate into practical reality.

But here comes Christmas, and Christmas persuades me that it is true. Christmas, the story of Christmas, has the ability to (once again) show me that no problem is too big for God. That it is really true that we can trust God even in the midst of our most trying circumstances, or most difficult challenges. Imagine a people under foreign occupation, whose line of kings has been cut off, who are forced to pay taxes to hated conquerors, who feel like they have failed to live up to all the promises of their founding fathers. They are suffering the indignity of national disaster—and with it all the very real problems that go along with not having political freedom. Their voices have been marginalized. They must curry favor with the Romans to get anything done, or to protect themselves. A foreign set of ideas and ideals is increasingly seeping into their mindset, and shaping the worldview of their children. If any people were facing very real problems, it was the first century Israelites. It would have been a bit like living in the Vichy Regime in France during World War 1, or living as a Christian in a country where the powers that be persecute Christians for their faith—a very real scenario faced by very real Christians today. But not only this existential despair, it would have also been easy for the Israelites at this time to despair *theologically*. God's prophets had spoken to them of their exile. And of their return from exile. But now what kind of return was this? Where was the God of their fathers? Were they still in 'exile'? Or had they now come back—and this, living under Roman occupation, was as good as it was going to get? It must have felt a very far distance from the glories of the realm of King David! What would Abraham, Moses or Isaac say about what happened to Israel, and how they went into exile? What hope was there for them now? All these insecurities, doubts, and very real sufferings were in the atmosphere in those days in Israel. And so Christmas tells us God took that problem and turned it into a solution!

I don't know what problems you are facing—perhaps they are personal; perhaps they are national or political. But Christmas tells us in no uncertain terms that no problem is too big for God. Turn to Him; turn from your sins and trust in Him. Israel's problems, their history, were all used by God to bring salvation through Christ to the globe. And your problem right now, whatever it is, could also be God's means of bringing salvation to many people! For no problem is too big for God.

4. The real Christ of Christmas saves me

We think of Christmas as a nice story, sweet, mild, tinkling little jingle bells. It is almost inevitable that we do—it is a story about a baby, and babies speak to our real if sometimes sentimental hopes for the future. I have no desire to remove from Christmas that feeling of hope and expectation. That is what Christmas is about, at least in part! We are looking forward to Christ's return, as well as celebrating His first coming. And so we have, rightly, a story that does have a sense of sweetness to it. Long may we be able to say with joy (and tears) 'Merry Christmas Everyone!' But while there is an inevitable, and not wrong, aspect of Christmas that might at times verge on the sentimental, even among the most theologically resolute of Christians, it is important to ensure that we have the real Christ of Christmas at the forefront of our minds. And Christmas, the more we understand it, shows us how this real Christ of Christmas saves us. We tend to forget but actually at that first Christmas time, or at least soon thereafter there was a massacre of babies under the aegis of the jealousy of wicked king Herod. That threat hangs in the background even over Bethlehem, as the wise men escape his conniving and then are warned to go back by a different route to avoid Herod. Christmas, and its joy, is not diminished by this sense of the spiritual battle around Christmas; it is heightened by it, we have more joy because of it. Christmas is not a story of the living room, the perfectly dressed, or the politely attired; it is a story of jealousy, hate, anger, death, mayhem, accusation, disaster—and how God saves sinners to bring life, hope, healing, joy, now and forevermore. How encouraging is this for those of us who are from time to time facing not the sweet quietness of a church late at night one Christmas Eve, but the mayhem of the Operating Room or the Emergency Room, or the cut throat world of business or politics. This real Christ of Christmas is the one who saves and gives us joy as He overcomes the enemies of God and brings us into His kingdom of joy now and forevermore.

A story

Brian was unsure how he'd get through this Christmas. Frankly, while he used to look forward to Christmas when he was a child now all he could do was pray to survive. Even the music annoyed him. All that upbeat slush, he said to himself. Over and over again. Everywhere he went there were reindeers and sleigh bells. It made him feel terrible—because it said he was supposed to be especially happy at this time of the year. Except he didn't feel in anyway happy whatsoever. In fact, he felt like an elf who'd got out of bed the wrong side, mislaid the presents he was working on, broken his tools, and got lost on the way to Santa's grotto. He felt terrible. It all began when he went through his divorce some years back. Before then he'd at least enjoyed some of Christmas. But now when he heard those Christmas songs coming, it made him feel sad. Sad for the family that he had lost, and annoyed that—if he was really honest with himself—everyone else was having such a good time.

The idea that Christmas could actually help him with his problems seemed a strange one to Brian. He was asked by a work colleague to come along to a Carol Service and while he was there he started to listen. Could it be that he was loved that much? Could it be that the answer lay not in a gift in a store but in The Gift in the manger in Bethlehem? Brian started to explore in his own mind and heart the real meaning of Christmas. And as he did so those songs that at first had seemed so annoying begun to take on new life. Especially the ones that were actually about Christmas, rather than just about sleigh bells. He especially liked Silent Night:

Silent night, holy night
   Son of God, love's pure light
Radiant beams from thy holy face
   With the dawn of redeeming grace

That 'dawn of redeeming grace' was shining light on Brian's path too now.

Questions for discussion

1. We don't like to think of our problems—much less discuss them with other people, unless we feel very safe in their company. But could you take a moment to think in your own head about what some of the challenges are that you face? This Christmas could you ask God to help you with those problems?

2. The Bible tells us that the root of our difficulties is sin. We are rebels against a holy God. We tend to think of sin as a very small thing, a light thing, a thing of no consequence. But to God sin is deadly serious. Would you confess any known sins to God and ask Him for forgiveness?

3. Perhaps you have a relational problem with another Christian believer. What does the humility of Christmas—and the forgiveness that is found for sinners at the cross of Jesus—teach us about the necessity of us forgiving other people?

4. How could you share the meaning of Christmas with a colleague or family member this Christmas? Is there a special event at church that you could invite them to?

5. When you look into the 'pure light', the 'dawn of redeeming grace', do you find that it puts your problems into a different perspective? How could you start to weigh your difficulties in the balance not of the supposedly better lives of other people, but instead in the balance of the eternal weight of glory that is for those who believe in Jesus?

Is Christmas Merely 'Chestnuts Roasting on an Open Fire'?

I like the traditional Christmas songs that you hear playing on the radio—most of them at least. But they can give the impression that Christmas is merely sentimental. When you hear Bing Crosby (yet again), or Mariah Carey, or whatever the latest Christmas album will be this year, the feeling you are left with is that Christmas is a feeling. A sentimental feeling, a feeling of good will, sleigh bells in the snow, reindeer with blinking red noses, snow falling like a cozy little blanket, and, yes, 'chestnuts roasting on an open fire'.

Is that all there is to it? No!

Most of the paraphernalia around Christmas—Christmas trees and the like—have nothing to do with the meaning of Christmas, and are nowhere to be found in the Bible. Christmas trees were brought into the English-speaking world by Prince Albert in Victorian England, importing the tradition from his native Germany. They may (or may not) have pagan origins; they didn't have that meaning to Albert, and they certainly don't have that meaning to most people today. They are a rather mild, harmless, heartwarming (usually) tradition.

Similarly, there are no reindeer in the Bible, there are no snowflakes at Christmas, no elves, and—*Spoiler Alert*—*Warning to parents: you might want to read the rest of this paragraph before sharing with your child*—no Santa Claus (or Father Christmas) in the Bible. Actually, though, Santa Claus is based upon a real person who really, we think, existed. St. Nicholas (or Santa Claus) was an ancient Christian bishop who made a name for himself by distributing gifts to poor children around Christmastime—hence the legend—though he never wore red boots or climbed down chimneys.

No, Christmas is not sentimental; it is *instrumental*. Certainly, the traditional sweet songs, trees and lights are all fine in their place, but actually Christmas is not just a sweet feeling. Christmas is not a sentiment; it is an instrument of *change*. The world was going in one direction; after Christmas it went in a different direction. The whole world. Everything changed after Bethlehem. The Roman Empire changed. Jerusalem changed. The Middle East changed. The Whole World changed because of Christmas—not the sort of thing that has ever happened (as far as I know) as a result of Bing Crosby songs on the radio (though they are perfectly fine in their own way if you like that kind of thing).

If you actually receive the message of Christmas this year, you will not, then, simply have a brief, momentary, pleasant warm glowing feeling.

Your life will change. Forever. The world around you will change. Forever. Your attitude will change. Your perspective will change. And your destiny.

How? It all starts with humility. The humility to recognize that the instrument that God will use to change your life, to change the world, to change the course of human history, to change countries, nations, families, businesses, is found ...

In a manger,

In a stable,

In the middle of nowhere.

And the instrument that God will use to bring your life into line with His amazing dream for you is the humility of Jesus, and the humility to accept Jesus as your Lord and Savior.

In many ways the real culture and message of Christmas stands as the last great bulwark and barrier against the culture and message of the celebrity. Nowadays, being at the top and being renowned is more and more celebrated as the be all and end all of life. Everyone not only wants to rule the world, everyone wants to be famous—or at least be recognized, at least be a celebrity. We live in the anti-humility age; the age where humility is believed to be more of a disorder or disease than a virtue to be pursued. Christmas then becomes merely sentimental not instrumental; not a place of change. But when we really look at the real meaning of Christmas our celebrity culture is challenged by a Christmas culture. Where were the great and the good when Jesus was born? Where were the accolades? Where was the palace? Where were the fine clothes and fancy dresses and the paparazzi recording the event to be broadcast around the world? Everything in the stable stinks of humility. It reeks of meekness. It has a stench of counter-cultural grace. If we will receive it as it truly was, and the message of Christmas as it truly is.

What's the difference between a sentimental Christmas and an instrumental Christmas—a Christmas that is used by God as a tool to bring us great joy as we center our lives on Christ? Here are some ways to help you think this through:

1. An instrumental Christmas is not merely an end point

We tend to think of Christmas as a season. We talk of the spirit of Christmas. Or, of course, Christmas Day. But what would it be like to consider how we can introduce the theology and spirit of Christmas to everyday life? There is a certain warm sweetness that comes from centering our lives upon the Christ of Christmas. There is a joy. And a peace. One way these feelings move beyond mere sentimentality is through moving beyond the mere season of Christmas. Think of Christmas this year not as an end point but as a starting point. What can you learn from Christmas that you can put into practice the rest of the year? Think of the presents you are giving not merely as things to give that will last only a few days, but things that will help people orientate their lives around Christ-centered life change. Why only sing Christmas songs at Christmas? There are some beautiful carols that we could sing at other times of the year too! Why not plan a mini-Christmas in early February, right when we are perhaps ready for winter to end (if we live in the Northern Hemisphere). Not a Christmas of gifts and a tree. But a mini-Christmas with some family and friends focused on the joys of Christ! Those are just some ideas. But the point is to think through ways that Christmas this year could be not an end point but a starting point towards growing Christlikeness in your life. Could you pray to that end?

2. An instrumental Christmas is also not merely an experience.

True Christianity is experiential (or what the Puritans used to call 'experimental'). It means knowing Christ personally yourself, and experiencing Him in your own life. But there is a certain kind of 'experience' which is more superficial; we experience a football game, or a good movie. Afterwards, we probably don't remember much about either. It was a good experience, but it didn't do much to us. We get used to having experiences which don't change our lives, or challenge us, or grow us in any significant way. But an instrumental Christmas will be more than this. Capture the teaching in the sermons by taking notes. Get a special journal for the Christmas season and write down what God is teaching you this year at Christmas so you can refer back to it later. As you prepare for the New Year—when many people make New Year's Resolutions—perhaps this year you could start earlier in that regard and do something a little more substantial. Could you make three Christmas Resolutions? What can you do to put into practice some of the Spirit of Christmas in your life? Is there someone with whom you need to find reconciliation—to live at peace with all people as far as it lies within your power to do so? Is there a particular habitual sin for which you need to ask God for forgiveness, and renewed power to dig out the root and repent of it and forsake it once again? Is there a particular calling that God has on your life, an area of service in the church, some spiritual gift that has lain dormant that you need to fan into flame? In other words, don't just let Christmas wash over you. Drink of the water of life this Christmas, and let the Spirit of Christ (which is the real spirit of Christmas) transform you and help you to take some new steps to live in newness of life this Christmas.

3. An instrumental Christmas is not merely a tradition

There are many traditions that have grown up around Christmas that people enjoy, and that can be sweet and pleasant. There is no point banning all tradition, for soon enough you will have simply replaced the old traditions with new traditions! There is a comfort to the repeated patterns that families (and churches) have at Christmas. Nothing wrong with that. But Christmas is not merely a tradition. Christmas is a transformation. You might like to take a moment, then, to examine your Christmas traditions and see whether they all fit within the pattern of the biblical norms of Christmas. Some people have grown into a tradition of drinking too much alcohol at Christmas—excusing it on the special holiday season. As if it were not ironic that holidays (or literally 'holy' days) were being used to excuse non-holy behavior! Some people have religious traditions which, while perhaps not specifically heretical and not thereby determinedly 'wrong,' nonetheless do not underline and emphasize the real meaning of Christmas. Do we tend to sing songs that are full of Christmas truth, or songs that are 'Christmassy' but not much about Christ? There can be a lot of sentimentality that grows up around traditions. It can seem a dangerous thing to touch a tradition, let alone change a tradition. But if we want Christ to be fully honored in our lives this Christmas, it is important that we ask whether the traditions, patterns and habits that we have adopted fully represent Him in a faithful way, or whether they somehow detract from the message of the true Christ?

4. An instrumental Christmas is not merely about 'going to church'

Going to church at Christmas is very important. Going to church as a Christian is an essential component of what it means to be a Christian: we are not to give up meeting together as the book of Hebrews puts it. But we can sometimes fall into the trap of thinking that if we have gone to church at Christmas then we have done all that we need to do, and we can cross 'Christmas' off our list. But remember where Jesus was born. He was not born in a palace or a castle. Neither was He born in a church or a cathedral. He was born in a stable. Christmas tells us of a message that is transformative not only for church as it meets together as the gathered church, but also for God's people as they go about their work and life outside of the four walls of the church building. For shepherds in the fields. For wise men. For a young couple trying to figure out where to have their new baby. Christmas speaks of the God who cares about the outcast, the lonely, those who don't feel that they fit into the 'inn' of institutional religion. Perhaps this Christmas, then, you could make a different kind of list. Not a list of who has been 'naughty or nice' in a legalistic-institutional-religion sense. But a list of how the gospel of Christ this Christmas applies to how you live your life outside of church. What does Christ's humility teach you about how to serve your wife, or your husband, your children, or your grandparents? What does Mary's willingness to do what God wanted teach you about how to follow God's commands even when they bump up against your preferences? What does Joseph's willingness to do what God asked him to do teach you about following God even if others around you don't approve, or sneer, or think that believing that Christ is the Savior of the entire world is not politically correct?

Christmas is far more than merely a sentimental time of year. Christmas is a tool that God can use—His instrument—to transform us to be the kind of people we were made to be, and to live the life of peace and joy that all those carols sing about.

A story

Jill loved Christmas. She loved the lights—always had done ever since she was a child. Each year her and her father would a special Saturday morning putting up all the lights around the house. It was a special memory, a sweet memory. And so whenever she drove through her town and began to see the lights turn on for the Christmas, something inside her glowed warmly. She liked Christmas.

But what she did not like was all this attempt by the (what she called in her mind) 'religious freaks' trying to turn Christmas into something more 'meaningful'—something that to her just seemed to spoil it. What's wrong with just enjoying Christmas? Can't it just be a good time? There are precious few times of the year when people go out to the pub, enjoy a few drinks, have a good old office party bash, and generally relax and have a good time. Why does it all have to be so serious? Why do they (those 'religious freaks') keep on wanting to put the 'Christ' back into Christmas? Oh she knew that originally Christmas had been a celebration of the birth of Jesus. Of course. But can't we now, these days, just get on with it, enjoy the traditions, eat the food, get and give the presents, and party together in a brief season of fun? Why spoil it by trying to make more of it?

At one of the office parties one year, though, Jill got talking to someone who worked with her called Sarah. This other colleague, Sarah, seemed to be rather quiet. Jill wanted to make sure she was alright. Oh yes, said Sarah, very much alright. You don't seem to be having a good time, Jill said. But I am, said Sarah—and I'm really waiting for this party to be over so I can get back to church and go to the Carol Service. That's such a wonderful service.

The idea that someone could be waiting for a party to be over so they could hurry off to church was a new idea for Jill. While she was still thinking about that, Sarah invited Jill to come with her. For some reason, before she could think of a good excuse, Jill found herself heading to church.

Well! That service was not what Jill had expected. Yes, it was, in a way, more serious. But there was something… how could she express it? Something profound. Something better. It had a taste of—and Jill hated to use this word but it came out of her mouth unbidden when she was walking back to her apartment after the service—transcendent. That was the word: transcendent. It spoke of the real joy, the higher pleasure, the greater experience. Jill wanted to find out more about that. It was a lot more than just chestnuts roasting on an open fire.

Questions for discussion

1. What could you do to make Christmas more meaningful for your family? Could you have an advent calendar with Bible verses in it and open one each day leading up to Christmas? Could you spend a special—even if brief—time praying before you open the presents, thanking God for His grace?

2. Compare Matthew 1:23 with Matthew 28:20. How does the promise of Christ's presence—Himself the very presence of God, the 'Immanuel' of Christmas—encourage you, motivate you, and exhort you to live for him more fully and more clearly as His representative?

3. Read through the well-known Christmas carol 'Hark the Herald Angels Sing.' With a piece of card or paper cover up the words of the carol and reveal them slowly one line at a time. Reflect on the meaning of each of those sentences as you read through the Carol. What sort of insights do you receive about the greater meaning of Christmas from this exercise?

4. Write on a piece of paper, or on your computer, or in your journal, for five minutes in free-flow stream-of-thought consciousness about the greater and biblical meaning of Christmas. Do you find that there are areas of the biblical story of Christmas that you need to learn more about? Are there parts of the biblical story that you haven't reflected on recently?

5. Before you go to church this Christmas, specifically ask God to help you see more of the message of Christmas.

QUESTION 3

How Can Christmas Make Me Happy Forever?

Christmas is meant to be a happy time, as all the commercials, music and stores tell us over and over again. The movies around Christmas encourage us that we can be happy now—we can forget real life for a little bit at least. If we do not enter into the 'Christmas spirit,' then we are a 'Scrooge,' or like the Grinch we are trying to 'steal Christmas.' Christmas is a happy time, we are told. There is certainly some truth to that. Lots of us look forward to Christmas immensely. We gather with our families. We enjoy the time to be away from work and school, to relax, chill, lie back and take life easy for a little bit.

But actually Christmas is not just about us being happy for a few days. Usually after Christmas there is a big feeling of letdown. We have opened all the presents. We have drunk all the eggnog we can stomach for another year. We cannot listen to yet another rendition of 'Rudolph the Red Nosed Reindeer' without feeling nauseated. And it's all over—we were 'happy' for a moment, perhaps, but that's it. Now we have to take all the decorations down, store them in the basement or attic, and look forward to snow for a month or two or three, before we enter into spring.

But Christmas is more than that. Actually in Christmas there is the secret to be happy *forever* (eternal joy). It requires three simple (not simplistic) steps.

1. Radical Repentance

If God, in His infinite wisdom, decides that the solution to all our problems is to become a man, to be born as a child, grow up, live in humility and mercy, die on a cross, rise again, ascend on high—if all this is His way to provide us with eternal life, joy and peace, then our response cannot be superficial.

Imagine if someone you knew decided that they were going to do something for you. Here's what they did: they got pregnant. They carried the baby to term. They brought the baby to you. They put him in a little basket, left him by the front door, rang the bell, and when you opened the door you found the newborn with a note attached.

The note said, 'We felt you needed help to be eternally happy, so we decided to give you this child to grow up, live and die for you. He's all yours. He's your savior.'

How would you respond? Not a dry eye. Not a superficial moment in sight. You would be horrified, amazed, stunned.

It would certainly cause you to change your life. You would never be the same again.

Christmas is saying that the way to be happy forever with God is to live a completely new life with God as your King. That is radical repentance. 'Radical' means 'by or from the root.' It is the opposite of superficial. It means deep down inside, from the basis of your philosophy of life, to your attitude, to every part of you, there is now a life of change. 'Repentance' means thinking differently. It's a new mindset, not just intellectually, but your whole attitude and shape of your life and will, all that is you is headed in a new direction. *Radical change.* That's the way to be happy forever, living now with Christ as your King.

For instance, this Christmas you might decide that instead of just 'going with the flow', the very message of Christmas requires you to do some good hard thinking and conduct a 'life review.' You might say that your life is summarized as Labor, Influence, Finance, Expertise. To what extent are you using these aspects of your life for Christ and His kingdom? Are you giving your hard work or *labor* for the advance of the kingdom? Are you using your *influence* with your friends, family, business contacts for the kingdom? Are you using your *finances* for the kingdom, not being just a tipper or even a tither but a resource of the kingdom with gospel generosity? Are you using your *expertise* for the kingdom—your skills, your spiritual gifts? If you are good at cooking, are you using that for the kingdom? If you are good at serving on committees, are you using that for the kingdom? If you are good at landscaping are you using that for the kingdom? In other words, when you look at the baby this Christmas, consider what sort of LIFE change it requires of you to follow Him in the coming year.

2. New Birth

The way to be happy forever is to have Christ born in your heart, by His Holy Spirit. This is the message of Christmas. Christmas is not just a message that 'Jesus was born in a stable.' Christmas is a message that God in Christ by His Spirit can be born in you. He can change your life so that you are born from above, born again, experience the new birth. This is the work of the Spirit; it is the gift of God, not earned by you, for which you can only ask, and which God promises He will give to all those who genuinely repent. The great Church of England minister, John Stott once wrote,

> We know that to find God and to accept Jesus Christ would be a very inconvenient experience. It would involve the rethinking of our whole outlook on life and the readjustment of our whole manner of life. And it is a combination of intellectual and moral cowardice which makes us hesitate. We do not find because we do not seek. We do not seek because we do not want to find, and we know that the way to be certain of not finding is not to seek.

So often we do not have the experience of Christ that we could have—and in fact do not find Christ at all—because deep down we really wish to avoid Him. *'We do not seek because we do not want to find, and we know that the way to be certain of not finding is not to seek.'* Would you instead this Christmas seek the new life that can only come through faith in the baby born at Christmas, the Savior? Jesus Himself put this condition very simply:

> Truly, truly, I say to you, unless one is born again he cannot see the kingdom of God (John 3:5).

It is the essential precondition of new life—the new birth by the Spirit. Ask Him for that new birth, seek Him, trust Him, put your faith in Him. Faith, not a notional mental assent, but a submission to His way and His will, to let God be God in your life. As Jesus famously put it later in that same chapter of John's gospel:

> For God so loved the world, that he gave his only Son, that whoever believes in him should not perish but have eternal life (John 3:16).

It is worth specially emphasizing this essential nature of the new birth—or regeneration—because in recent years its emphasis has often been replaced by a tendency to equate the language of being 'born again' with a political or cultural affiliation. But when Jesus uses the language of being born again, He is not referring to our political party, or our view on various cultural matters; He is referring to spiritual new birth. This emphasis on the new birth is not a new idea formulated by mid-twentieth century revivalistic preachers. It goes back to Jesus. To the gospels. To the manger itself. It has frequently been urged on by leading Christians, preachers, and indeed poets. The great Victorian poet Alfred Tennyson famously sighed,

> Ah for a man to arise in me
> That the man I am may cease to be.[1]

Perhaps that's your sigh. You long to be able to put off old patterns of behavior, bad habits and unworthy thoughts. You long to be clean and pure. You long to be able to start again and have the power to be new. All

---

1   Maud, https://www.bartleby.com/42/6491.html

this comes through the message of Christmas. More than that, it comes through the *person* of Christmas, the Christ of Christmas. Maybe it was never better put than in the famous carol 'O Little Town of Bethlehem':

O holy child of Bethlehem
Descend to us, we pray
Cast out our sin and enter in
Be born to us today
We hear the Christmas angels
The great glad tidings tell
O come to us, abide with us
Our Lord Emmanuel.

3. New Life

With a new birth comes a whole new life. It opens up in front of you now. There will be difficulties inevitably—we live in a world that is far from perfect. But whereas before you were wandering aimlessly, uncertain, now you are set on a trajectory of meaning, purpose and destiny, whereby everything is new, and one day all things will be new. You will weep, but not without meaning. You will hurt, but not without purpose. Your life is new: a new start, new day, new every moment, for a new purpose, to be a part of the new heavens and the new earth when Christ comes again to rule in power, glory and majesty.

That LIFE—Labor, Influence, Finance, Expertise—now has meaning and purpose to it. Of course, you might think that if God is Sovereign then my life must by definition be fulfilling God's purposes. He is, after all, in control. Who am I to talk back to God? What will be will be, and I will do what He wants in the end. But here we are talking about a different kind of purpose, a purpose now of joy and meaning—not resistance and rebellion and ultimate final misery. The famous Oxford Professor C. S. Lewis put it like this,

> A merciful man aims at his neighbor's good and so does 'God's will', consciously co-operating with 'the simple good'. A cruel man oppresses his neighbor, and so does simple evil. But in doing such evil, he is used by God, without his own knowledge or consent, to produce the complex good—so that the first man serves God as a son, and the second as a tool. For you will certainly carry out God's purpose, however you act, but it makes a difference to you whether you serve like Judas or like John.

Now, in Christ and because of Christ—and Christmas—you can serve like John, like who you were made to be, in fullness of life and in fulfilment of your destiny and true desires. We are never freer than when we submit. The real slave is the one who rebels against their Designer's purpose and against the Designer Himself. But once you align yourself to His will and His goals for your life, then your purpose becomes His purpose, and you have a growing sense that 'you were made for this' (for you were).

That's my desire for you, that you would find this Christmas season such a renewed joy and peace, that your experience of Christmas goes beyond the merely temporary and passing. And it becomes a fulfilling life for you, your family, your children, your friends and eternity.

That's how Christmas can make you happy forever: Radical Repentance, New Birth, New Life.

A story

Bill never thought much of Christianity. He hadn't grown up in a Christian home. And for him the Christian story seemed to be for wimps. Nietzsche's criticism that Christianity had neutered the West of its masculinity and power resonated with him. He didn't want all that sort of 'die-to-yourself' and 'take up your cross' stuff. Not for him. He wasn't going to be anyone else's stepping stone to their agenda. He was no wall flower. If someone needed confronting, he'd confront them. If someone needed putting back in their place, he was more than happy to oblige. Mind you he didn't thrust himself on other people, either. Live and let live was his motto. But he was not interested in any religious groveling to other people—much less to some cryptic sublime being in the sky who didn't seem much interested in him anyway. Why should he worship God? Was God so insecure that He needed people to worship Him? Why couldn't God—if He existed—leave us all alone? No, it was all too pathetic and weak for him. He was a protector. He looked out for the little guys, the weak ones, and protected them against the wolves in the world. But to do that he had to be tough. And he didn't have any time for submission and turning the other cheek. He'd rather punch back if he was punched.

One time, Bill was asked to go to a nativity service by one of his neighbors. He decided to go along because he liked him. Besides he wanted to make sure that this church wasn't taking advantage of his friend. The church seemed a bit too intense and enthusiastic. He wasn't at all sure it wasn't really a cult.

Well, if they asked him for any money he wasn't going to give them any. And if he spotted any Kool-Aid drinkers, cult members, any love-bombing cultic techniques, he'd be out of there pretty quick, and he'd drag his friend with him for his own good too.

Then, for someone he wasn't sure exactly why, as he stood in front of that nativity. That crib. The Baby Jesus. Something struck him. There as a note written under it that he felt drawn to read. It said simply: 'Imagine this: The God of all glory came to save you.' He kept on looking at that baby, and he kept on thinking. Could it really be true? If it was, he knew it would be enough to make him happy—not just about what's happening, but truly joyful—forever. Here was someone who hadn't played the game of the survival of the fittest but had actually given His life for someone else.

Questions for discussion

1. The wise men bowed and worshipped at the manger. Have you experienced the joy of worshipping Christ?

2. Happiness is a natural human response to what is happening. Joy, however, is spiritual fruit of a relationship with Jesus whatever is happening. Do you have joy? Do you have a relationship with Jesus?

3. The Bible tells us that Christ Jesus came into the world to save sinners. Will you turn from your sin and put your trust in Jesus? You don't have to be perfect. In fact, you need to admit that you're not! Trust him. And be saved.

4. Joy comes from putting Jesus first. It is spelt J.O.Y—Jesus, then Others, then You. A lot of people find they have little joy because they put themselves first—all they have is Y.O.J. (not J.O.Y.)! What could you do to serve Christ this Christmas? Ask God to show you.

5. Perhaps you are going through a very difficult time personally as you read this. If you are struggling, let me encourage you to seek a pastor or Christian counselor for advice and help. There are times when all of us need someone to come alongside and help us see things in the right perspective. Look at that baby Jesus. Given for you. How can you keep that perspective in focus this Christmas?

QUESTION 4

Is Christmas Just Getting 'Cool Stuff'?

What will be the latest gizmo this Christmas? As I write, the leading candidates appear to be iPhone, iPad and Android phones. Perhaps a particular video game? Perhaps a new cool toy for children under five? Perhaps you will have an opportunity for something more expensive, or dramatic?

It is easy for those of us who live in Western countries to compare ourselves with people who live down the road from us, or across the tracks from us, or people we see on TV and in Hollywood, and think that we are relatively less well off than other people. The reality is that many of us are far wealthier than the vast majority of people in the entire world. You gain this sense pretty amazingly when you travel for a little bit in an impoverished country, or live there for a while, and then come back to a Western country and enter a grocery store. The first time you do that it is almost mind blowing. You just cannot conceive of the amount of choice, selection, bright colors and opportunity laid before you in any one of

35

several grocery stores in your town—until you compare it with what is on offer in a shantytown outside Johannesburg (for instance).

And that is just talking about groceries.

When you compare impoverished areas with what we have, not on our tables to eat, but the amount of money that is spent on 'cool stuff' (gizmos, gadgets, technology, games etc.), you can begin to feel turned off by the commercialization of Christmas, or the commercialization of life in general. Surely life is more than what you can buy in a store? Or through Amazon. com at special reduced prices on Black Friday after Thanksgiving? Surely life is more than that; surely Christmas is more than that.

But what? Most of us have heard the story of Bethlehem, the wise men, Mary and the angels, and all the rest many times, but when it actually comes down to our celebration of Christmas, it all seems to center on opening presents on Christmas Eve, or Christmas morning, and that means that much of Christmas seems to be the stress of finding presents, getting presents, giving presents. In short, 'cool stuff.' Could there be more to Christmas than it being the season of 'giving and receiving' (which it seems = the season of giving and getting 'cool stuff')?

Think about the actual word 'Christmas.' What does it mean? It is composed of two parts: 'Christ' and 'mas.' The word 'mas' comes from the Latin for the close of the traditional communion service. At the end it is said *ite missa est*, which means something like 'go; it is the dismissal.' The 'mas' part of Christmas is what remains from the end of that seasonal communion service. It suggests a worship dimension to Christ-*mas*. The word 'Christ' means 'Messiah' which means 'Anointed One' who was the 'King.' Those who were kings were anointed as kings. Jesus is The Christ; that is, He is The

36

Anointed One; that is, He is the promised King who has come to rule God's way and as God. He has come to establish God's kingdom. That kingdom is now being proclaimed (at *Christ*-mas), so that those who believe can enter the kingdom. One day that kingdom will be fully and finally established when Jesus returns. So 'Christ-mas' means 'King-worship'. Christmas is about worshipping Jesus as King.

It is a feast. A celebration. All worship has a celebration aspect to it. You are not worshipping something (or someone) when you do not enjoy it, love it, become excited by it, long to tell others about it. Worship is saying, 'Wow, this is amazing! I love this; isn't this great! Come and find out more about this and experience what I have experienced.'

So we celebrate at Christmas. We give gifts. We receive gifts. We enjoy Christmas—we are not Scrooges or Grinches. We lavish upon Christ our hearts' affections. We love Him. We love each other. We rejoice! *Because* we are worshipping Christ as King.

It's like after someone has won a gold medal, been elected to office, or been crowned king. If you think that is a great thing to have happened, you will celebrate. You will tell everyone how worthy that person is to have won the medal, been elected to office, or been crowned king. Similarly, at Christmas we rejoice, celebrate, enthuse, proclaim, declare, make merry, because it is *Christ-mas*. It is the feast of Christ the King.

How can you make the most of Christmas this year as a 'feast of Christ the King'?

1.   Look at your schedule and prioritize Christmas carol services and events that lift up the name of Jesus. You have to be proactive here. So often our schedule gets filled with things that are running toward

other people's agendas or ideas. Christmas is such a busy time of year for many people. It can soon become not the time of goodwill to all people, but the time of running around like a headless chicken with endless 'Christmas-y' appointments. Look at the opportunities you have and prioritize based upon what is most exalting of Christ, in particular what will give you opportunities to invite other people to church and to hear the gospel. One of the great dangers in our day and age is distraction. We have so many opportunities, so many things that we could do. But if we want to make sure that this year Christmas is focused upon Christ, then it starts with our schedule, our calendar, what we actually do. And, in order to manage that, you need to proactively look ahead and plan in those events that are most reflective of the real meaning of Christmas.

2. Why not set aside a special few hours this year simply to read through the Christmas story? Perhaps you are very familiar with that story. Or perhaps it is new to you. Either way, don't receive it all second hand. Get a Bible—in a modern translation—pick one of the gospel stories of the birth of Christ. And read it. Have a notebook beside you and write down what you observe. You'll find that new things will jump off the page at you as you read the Bible prayerfully with a humble spirit, ready to receive. What do you observe that is surprising? Write that down. What do you observe that is a challenge? Write that down. What do you observe that you need to apply to your own life? What do you observe that is encouraging? What do you observe that you could share with someone else? Then having read through

the Christmas story once for observations, now go back through and see what kind of applications there are for you. Remember: the Bible never has an application now that contradicts the meaning it would have had when it was first written. This is why it is important to read the story as a whole, in context. Ask the classic Bible reading questions: what does it say? What does it mean? What does it mean for me? What is there that you need to repent of? What is there that you need to ask for God's help to put into practice? Read through the Christmas story in the Bible, prayerfully and humbly, asking that God would open your eyes to wondrous things in His Word.

3. Make sure you celebrate! Christmas is meant to be a time of joy. But it is easy for 'earnest' Christians to only ever be serious and committed, and not often joyful or even playful. Celebrate the Christ! There is a lot to celebrate. I know that parents of young children, in particular, can find it very hard to find the time to do anything other than crawl into bed exhausted at the end of a long day. Still, even then, make sure you take a moment—if you can only find that—to celebrate. For instance, sing your favorite carol. You can find good examples of Christmas carols on the internet. You'll find the words there. Read it and even sing it. You may not have a voice that would fit into a choir of angels—but what does it matter? Make a joyful noise unto the Lord, even if your neighbors might think it most definitely is a 'noise'! Or give something special, receive a special gift. We can think of Christmas as being so overtaken by materialism that we forget the original purpose of giving and receiving gifts. Which is to celebrate!

And to remember that it is by grace—God's unmerited favor, a gift—that we receive God's salvation. It does not have to be an expensive gift. It could even be something you make yourself, rather than buy. But something that expresses a spirit of joy, of celebration.

4.   And of course if it is a feast, then enjoy—if you can—some good food. There are many people who are hungry. If you are someone reading this who does not have access to regular food, I encourage you to go to your local church or a soup kitchen of one kind or another and you will, I pray, find people who will help you and give you something special to eat even at Christmas. But for many of us, we can be so nervous about putting on weight with food—another danger, to be sure!—that we forget to celebrate Christmas through a literal feast. If heaven itself, according to Jesus, is a banquet, that why not have a banquet at Christmas! Perhaps you remember the scene in C. S. Lewis' *The Lion, the Witch, and the Wardrobe* where Father Christmas finally makes his way into Narnia, and the winter snow disappears, and the Narnians celebrate with a feast. Such is the feast of Christmas: an opportunity to receive the grace of God, through repentance of our sins, openhearted humility, before the King of Kings and Lord of Lords!

Christmas, then, is far more than just 'getting cool stuff.' It is a feast, a celebration, a moment of transcendent joy, as we reflect upon and receive in our hearts, the real meaning of Christmas, the Christ born king.

A story

Jane had always enjoyed Christmas presents. Who doesn't? she thought to herself. Ever since she was a child she had looked forward to that moment when she unwrapped the present and saw what was inside. Her mother had been a particularly enthusiastic gift-giver. That was part of it, perhaps. For Jane, presents were closely associated with her mother's and father's love. She loved presents because the presents seem to represent some sort of deeper meaning associated with love. There's nothing wrong with that, she would protest to anyone who suggested that her love of gifts, presents, material rewards was a little bit out of hand. Jane could never throw away gifts. Once something had been given to her—however useless it became—she could never pass it on to someone else, much less re-gift it or resell it. Over the years, her house became packed with presents. The basement was filled with the presents that she could no longer find room for in the main rooms in the house. And still each Christmas, what she really got excited about—if she was honest—was not the 'spiritual' meaning of Christmas, but the much more tangible benefits of a new sweater, a new pair of shoes, a special box of chocolate, or something more expensive. As she grew older, she found she needed more impressive gifts to scratch the same 'present-gift' itch that in earlier years had been satisfied by a new doll or a new dress. Now she wanted a really expensive dress. Some unique piece of art. Jewellery of course.

One Christmas, though, she looked at the presents she had received and realized it was not enough. That such a litany of material benefits was not what she was really looking for. And she began to ask deeper questions. She started to read the Bible (again). She started to want to experience Christ through His

Word—to know Him personally and be in relationship with Him. She started— bit by bit—to focus on The Gift. Could it be that her desire for 'gifts' was just a pale reflection of the One Great Gift, of Jesus Christ, and His grace for her? Jane was beginning to think that her desire for gifts was not too great, but too small. And really she should desire something—Someone—higher and better than any mere human, material, gift.

Questions for discussion

1. What was you favorite ever Christmas gift? What made that gift so special to you?

2. Why do you think the tradition of giving and receiving gifts has developed at Christmas? What deeper giving and receiving does the gift-giving at Christmas represent?

3. Have you personally received the gift of Jesus into your heart by faith? Do you know the grace, or the gift, of God?

4. Do you think it is wise to limit the amount of money that you spend on gifts?

5. What could you do this Christmas to give towards the work of the gospel in your church and around the world?

QUESTION 5

Why Should I Care About Baby Jesus?

Sweet and mild, gentle and easy going, what is there not to like about 'Baby Jesus'? On the other hand, what sort of difference can 'Baby Jesus' really make to my life? And why should I care about Him in particular?

The story of the Bible is much more than 'Baby Jesus.' Jesus grew up, became a man, lived, died, and (Christians believe) rose again from the dead. He is more than 'Baby Jesus.' He did more. He said more. He lived more. He died, He rose, He reigns. He will return. He will judge the living and the dead.

At Christmas we do not just celebrate the cute, little, sweet 'Baby Jesus.' We remember the birth of a King. This Jesus became a man—fully God, fully man, in one person—for our sake to bring us to God.

He is presented at Christmas in stunning humility. The God of the whole universe condescended to be born in a stable, surrounded by poverty and immense indignity. It is the divinely designed technique to slip under the radar of our pride and appeal to us to turn to Him, believe in Him, and follow Him with all of our lives.

Humility, mercy, peace.

But not just a 'Baby Jesus.' He is born 'King Jesus.' His reign as King is now declared through His death and resurrection, and He offers us salvation—but if we reject Him, then He will return to judge.

Why should I care about 'Baby Jesus'? Because He's not just a baby. He's the King. He's the Lord of heaven and earth. *At His feet we fall.*

The message of Christmas, with all its sweetness, offers us hope. It silently pleads that we might let the Christ rule in our hearts, descend to us, and make us born anew, as He was born in that stable.

We should care because this offer is beyond anything that could be offered in this world. It is more important, longer lasting (nothing can beat eternity), more pleasurable ('pleasures forevermore'), more honoring to God.

We should care because this 'Baby Jesus' grew up, was crucified, died, was buried, rose again, and will return. When He returns He will not return as a baby. He will return in glory, and in judgment. And what will matter then is whether we have worshipped Jesus and accepted Him as our King, or whether we have rejected Him as 'nothing but a baby.'

Here are four life-changing reasons why we should care about 'Baby Jesus.'

1 First, the example it gives. We live in a world where self-assertion and self-attainment are everything. But what if the very focal point, the zone of worship, the center of all was not a celebrity. What if the greatest example that we are all meant to emulate humbled Himself and became obedient to

be born as a baby, and die for the sins of the world? What if—in short—our minds and hearts are shaped by the vulnerability, the sweet condescension, and the unerring humility, of this baby? It is such a powerful example.

Babies, human babies, of course, are not innocent. Anyone who has been a mother or father will tell you that babies can be difficult to handle sometimes! But what if there was a baby who was truly innocent. Never sinned. Pure and perfect. What if the God of the whole universe became, for us, a … baby. The sheer astonishing nature of that vast humility is enough to crack the hardest of hearts, if the Spirit softens. We say to each other sometimes (when we are facing a tough challenge and need to 'man up') 'don't be such a baby.' But what if the one who needs no pretension of strength—who is the Power behind power itself, and the Might behind all might—yet condescended to be born as a baby? What a lesson! What an example!

Why would we insist on our status and our honor, when we worship this one born in a manger? Think of it like this. Say you are observing two people arguing. One says to the other 'I deserve better than that.' The other says, 'Maybe, but then I did this and, really, I deserve it.' And on and on the argument goes. Say they are arguing about who is the best at, for instance, tennis and therefore deserves the last slot on the courts available. And as they argue about who is going to get the court that they both think they deserve, along comes the current world #1 on the professional tennis tour—and instead of insisting that he is the best tennis player, is quite happy to sit at the back, and take his turn in the line, and not be first, but be last. Those two who are arguing about being first? It seems ridiculous when you see the world #1 happy to wait his turn. In a much, much greater way, the Lord of All Glory sets us an example of humility by becoming a baby.

Second, the message it sends. Some people think that Christianity is a message of power and dominion. They think that Christianity is trying to assert its rule over other people. They think that all religions do this— and they see Christianity as just another religion. But here, if anywhere, surely here at the manger with the baby is a message that undermines that claim. How can anyone say that the Christian message is about colonial domination of peoples when at the heart of the message is a baby? Ever seen a baby go to war? Of course, babies can be demanding! But imagine a perfect baby. One who is not exerting his selfish will over an exhausted mother or father, but a pure innocent and morally righteous baby in every way. How can you think that such a baby is out to dominate you, or ruin your life, or control you? Some Christians argue as to whether the cross at Easter or the manger at Christmas is the more central aspect of the message of Christianity. But really they belong together: as early church leader Anselm put it long ago, without Christmas, Easter makes no sense. The message is not that *someone* died; it is that *He* died, the Lord of all glory. The incarnation is what makes the crucifixion work : as 'none but God *can* make and none but man *ought* to make, it is *necessary* for the God-man to make it.'[1] The heart of the Christian message is love: and that love is shown and exemplified and preached at the manger, and at the cross—where the God-man died that we might live. What a message! This is the message that transforms us and changes our lives.

---

1   *Cur Deus Homo*, chapter VI.

Third, the person He is. Think with me. At Christmas, this year, think not just about the sweet sentimentality of the season, but the extraordinary truth of who Jesus is that is being revealed. *Who God is.* What is your mental picture of God? What ideas or words come into your mind when you hear the word 'God'? The most important thing about any person is what they think when they hear the word God. That will define you more than anything else in your life. Do you think of God as love—and not holy? Do you think of God as judge—and not merciful? How balanced is your view of the God of the universe? Are you shaped by what culture says about God, or by what your parents taught you about God? What is the way to begin to bring our ideas about God into line with the reality? There is no better place to start than at Christmas. At the manger. Looking into the face of the baby. There He is. There HE is. What do you make of Him? Is this the God you worship? It is such a scandal for so many people. We all try at times to intellectualize it. How could the Creator of the entire universe be a baby? What does that mean? And as we ask such questions we are left to wonder—in love and praise and worship. The more we bang our head against the mystery of the incarnation, the more we realize that the idea of God cannot be contained in our mind. He is bigger and greater, and just like a two-dimensional being could not understand a three-dimensional object, so we are left speechless at the full and complete God in this baby.

Fourth, the person we become. Looking at baby Jesus is life-changing. Repenting from our arrogance, and sinful selfishness, and soulless pride, is life-changing. Trusting our lives to the one who made us is life-changing. There He is, as the carol puts it, silently pleading. He is not threatening you.

He is not attacking you. Will you have Him? Will you receive Him? Will you trust Him? Will you worship Him?

A story

Gary hadn't really given much thought to 'baby Jesus' for many years. Sure, he'd pass the occasional manger scene on his way to work. And some of his more religious friends would send him Christmas cards with a picture of baby Jesus on the front of the card. But for Gary, the whole 'baby Jesus' thing (as he liked to call it in his own mind) was odd. Why this excitement about a baby? Perhaps if you were a woman you'd get excited about a new-born baby, but Gary was very much a man's man—and he had very little time for all the paraphernalia and hassle that came along with little infants. Sleepless nights. Screaming. Dirt and chaos. No thanks, he said to himself. He looked at baby Jesus, and just saw a baby. And that didn't make him feel all 'warm gooey' inside; it made him feel… well, not much of anything at all, to be honest.

A friend of his—who Gary knew was (in Gary's way of thinking) very 'religious'—suggested to him that he was thinking about this 'baby Jesus' all from the wrong point of view. He suggested that he should read a very old book called Cur Deus Homo *(or 'Why God became Man') written by someone called Anselm. Surprisingly—at least to Gary—he found this book easily accessible online, and also surprisingly it didn't seem a very long book. He started to read it. When he came across this phrase, it made him stop and think:*

> none but God can make and none but man ought to make, it is necessary for the God-man to make it.

Why Should I Care About Baby Jesus?

Gary started to look at the baby Jesus differently from that moment on. He saw in baby Jesus not a sentimental attempt to grab at his hear strings, but a radical humility in love for His own redemption. What kind of God would do this? What kind of God would give Himself so thoroughly as to become obedient to take on the life of a human and give Himself to die on the cross for Gary's sins? The more Gary thought about it, the more Gary realized that this kind of God deserved his love, his wonder, his worship, indeed his whole life.

Questions for discussion

1. What do you think of when you look at a manger scene with baby Jesus?

2. Do you think that is what the apostle Paul thought of when he thought about Jesus' humanity? (See Phil. 2:5-11)

3. If God loves us this much—that He would send His only Son to be born as a man and die for us—what sort of love should we have towards Him?

4. Is contemporary Christianity mirrored in the self-sacrificial humility of the incarnation? How could we be more self-giving (and less self-asserting)?

5. Why do you think it so essential that we accept the full humanity and full divinity of baby Jesus?

QUESTION 6

What Is the Magic of Christmas?

Around Christmas many stores, movies and advertisements play off the idea of the 'magic' of Christmas. *Miracle on 34th Street*, the angel in *It's a Wonderful Life*, even the idea of 'paying it forward' by getting into the 'Christmas spirit' and paying for the coffee or car wash or groceries of the person behind you—all this can generate that magical Christmas feeling.

All this feels good, is sometimes entertaining and, in the case of the 'pay it forward' idea, beneficial and wholesome. But is it what Christmas is actually about?

Is Christmas about sentimental feelings?

Is Christmas about mysterious magical ideas (fairies and pixies and mythical beings)?

Is Christmas about being kind to one another?

Or is there more to it than that? Did the Son of God come to Bethlehem to teach us about how to live comfortable, kind, good lives? Or did He come to *do* something?

The radical message of Christmas is that we *will not understand it until we understand just how big the problem is*. If we do not grasp the issue at stake, the problem we face, then the real message of Christmas will seem inconceivable, petty, and even inconsequential. Just another myth.

The problem we face is that we are not only radically cut off from God by our sin, rebellion and opposition to God and His holy law—but that God must judge (as He is holy). And yet God is also loving.

A holy God is faced with rebels whom He loves. His solution is to be born as a man, live the perfect life, die the perfect death, and solve our alienation from God—as well as express perfectly the twin poles of His own character, love and justice. God loved us enough to send His Son. God was consistently holy to sacrifice His Son for us.

The magic, then, of Christmas is the magic of God making peace with us through the birth, life and death of Jesus Christ at the cross, the magic of reconciliation. Between us and God. It is the magic of God in Christ reconciling the world to Himself. This is not the magic of cute cards, seasonal stories, little pixies or Santa's elves. This is the True Magic of reconciliation.

If, then, you really want to experience the magic of Christmas, you will need to take two steps. First, you will need to accept God's offer of reconciliation by turning from your sins, bowing before King Jesus and accepting Him as Lord of your life. His Spirit will enter your heart and you will be born anew and start a whole new life.

The second step is to start to live as a reconciled person. That means seeking to help others be reconciled to Christ too, and being reconciled to them yourself, as well, where possible.

Put it like this: the True Magic of Christmas is forgiveness.

How can you experience that 'magic' this Christmas?

First, consider the truth. The magic that we tend to associate with the season of the holidays, or Christmas, is a kind of sentimentality, or fairy tales. It is easy for us to think that Christmas, even the real Christmas, lives in a similar never never land of myths and dragons and magical flying reindeer. But the first step in really experiencing the magic of Christmas this year is to consider that this story actually is true. It happened. It took place. It is not merely a story; it is a story that occurred. Perhaps you find it hard to accept that. Perhaps the story of Christmas seems to you to be incredible, as in un-believable. It is not something that—however much the Bible stories may *claim* it is true—you can really accept as actually true. The idea of the incarnation seems so extraordinary, so non-scientific, that for some people no matter how clear the explanation, or how great the evidence, it cannot, indeed should not, be believed. But consider the truth. Consider that if there is enough evidence then, however unlikely it is to have occurred, we may be convinced by the evidence that it did occur. Who would have thought a hundred years ago that someone could carry a talking device in their pocket, write messages that appear instantaneously on another talking device anywhere around the world? The world of the smartphone was hardly conceivable even thirty years ago. There is so much about life that we do not truly understand. How can we really say that the incarnation is impossible? Besides, when we are talking about God, we are talking about the one who, by definition, can do the impossible. This does not mean that if we accept a miracle like the incarnation we must accept that 'miracles happen all the time', and throw out the window the laws of science. It means that one time God did something so extraordinary that the very order that defines our universe, because it defines God's person, was held in abeyance, and was transcended and transformed by the incarnate Son of God.

Look at it like this: if it did not occur, then what did occur? This is the great question that those who doubt the Christ-story that Christmas introduces have to wrestle with. The world was transformed by a simple proclamation of the gospel of Jesus' birth, death and resurrection. If that is not true, then what is the alternative? Consider the truth. The magic of Christmas begins with the recognition that we are dealing with something that really happened.

Second, hear the message. There is a message of Christmas. The angels proclaimed it on that first Christmas Eve. It is a message of

- Good news

- Great joy

- For all the people

- About the King

- Who is Savior

- Who is Messiah

- Who is Lord

- Which means glory to God in the highest

- And peace on earth among those with whom He is pleased

Would you hear this message? Christmas is not just an event. It is not just a party. It is not just about presents. It is a message; it is good news. And Christmas is something that gives us not just temporary happiness, but the kind of joy that lasts through changing circumstances—and great joy at that. Christmas fulfills the promises of the King who is to come in the line of David. It tells us of one who comes to save us. He is the King. He is the Messiah. He is the Lord God. All this glorifies and honors God, and gives peace with God on earth to all with whom God is pleased.

What a message! How different are the many other messages we hear these days. Messages of conflict. Messages of confusion. Messages of hate and exclusion. Messages of tribal power battling for precedence. Messages of bitterness and deceit. But here is a different kind of message. Wow! Focus on this message. Focus on what Christmas *means*, and the magic of Christmas, through hearing the message of Christmas. Read through Luke 2:8-20 right now. See there the good news, the great joy, the glory to God, the peace on earth. Focus on the message. Hear that message again. Don't let it be drowned by what people *say* Christmas is about. Hear the actual message again.

Third, spot the sign. The sign that was given still speaks to us today. 'You will find a baby wrapped in swaddling cloths and lying in a manger' (Luke 2:12). There is much that is unusual about this sign. Who ever heard of a newborn baby lying in a manger—a feeding trough for animals? It was an unusual sign, something that would make you realize that what the angels were speaking about was coming true, something that would make you realize you had come to the right place when you saw it. There is something intrinsically unusual about this sign. But the counter-intuitive aspect of it continues still today. Who ever heard of the God of the universe humbling Himself and becoming obedient to be born as a man, even a little baby, in such a place of indignity? It tells us that Christmas is not what we think. It's not a religious trick or a sales technique to get us to buy into a new philosophy or religion. It tells us that God is not who many people say He is. He is not out to control us or dominate us or manipulate us. He came as a baby. What vulnerability; what humility; what grace and mercy.

Fourth, go and worship. The shepherds followed the direction of the angels, found the baby and returned praising God for all they had heard and seen. The magic of Christmas—the forgiveness and reconciliation, the peace and joy that Christmas offers comes as we receive the baby Jesus as King Jesus. As we bow and worship Him. Such praise of Jesus, such recentering of your life upon Jesus, such adoration, will change your life. It's a kind of true magic.

A story

Magic. John had always been fascinated by it. Whether Tolkien, C. S. Lewis' *Narnia stories, or* Harry Potter, *the thread that resonated with John was this idea and feeling of the magical. He liked to watch those 'magicians' who did magic tricks—the sleight of hands and the feint that tricked the audience into thinking that real magic was taking place. But even more than he liked the idea that there might actually be a true kind of magic somewhere. When he read C. S. Lewis'* The Magician's Nephew, *he found himself as interested in the different kind of rings that uncle Andrew had put together—as well as the thought that there was another world where magic really worked. Could it be? Could* there be a way of manipulating atoms and molecules, as well as thoughts and feelings, through saying the right words or waving your hands in the right way? The Star Wars idea of the force also intrigued him, for the same reason. All that meant that Christmas was a time of year that John particularly enjoyed. Very often movies and stories that had a magical element to them came out around Christmas. And there was a feeling in the air, in the atmosphere, at the time of the year of Christmas that often—at least to John—seemed, well, magical.

He was fascinated with the history of alchemy, and how some early Chemists had thought along more alchemist kind of lines; he found not just astronomy, but astrology interesting. Was the fate of us all read in the stars? What did it mean, for instance, that the wise men followed the star to find King Jesus? Were those wise men, or 'Magi' (from which we get our word 'magic'), only precursors, or original magicians? Did they use alchemical arts, or even astrology to find the time when Jesus was born? Were they descendants from the magical wise men that Daniel had lived among, and did they learn from Daniel of the prophecies of the one who was to come?

The more John delved into the some of these ideas, the more two contrary thoughts came to be clear in his mind. On the one hand, some of it seemed quite dangerous. Demonic, even. John, wanted nothing to do with that kind of 'magic.' And yet could there be, as Aslan famously put it in The Lion, the Witch and the Wardrobe, a 'deeper' magic—the real thing, the essence of all things, the Word who became flesh? Increasingly, he began to realize that the Bible was not a mere intellectual tome of religious history, but a living book that spoke of how to have a relationship with God Himself. And as John put his trust simply and purely in Christ, he began to realize that Christ was the one he had been looking for all along.

Questions for discussion

1. Do you find the season of Christmas magical? If so, why? If not, why not?

2. Do you think there is a sort of 'deeper magic' to Christianity?

3. Have you encountered the real Christ of Christmas? Do you have a story to tell of how Jesus met you and changed you?

4. What is wrong about the contemporary desire for magic? How can you speak against that?

5. In what way could you experience forgiveness of sins this Christmas—both for yourself, and in how you forgive other people?

QUESTION 7

Can I Have Christmas All Year Round?

I hope not! If Christmas means that mad frantic rush to buy enough presents, put up the decorations, make sure Aunt Mildred has all she needs for Christmas Day, preparing the food etc. etc.—well, then living like that *every day* is probably not to be desired. It would drive you mad, give you a hernia, cause unending tension, and (no doubt), in the end, be boring. Holidays are all fine and good, but after a while you want to move on with life.

On the other hand, there are some aspects of Christmas which many of us enjoy, and probably would want to be more permanent fixtures in our lives. We tend to have a feeling of sweet merriment at Christmas, a tendency to be kind to each other, and a sense of something exciting to look forward to. This, I suppose, is the sort of sentiment that people mean when they say that they wish every day could be Christmas Day. They wish that they could open presents (and the presents would be ones that they wanted), that they could have food they enjoyed in plentiful supply, that they did not have to work at something unpleasant, that they could be with their family. They might even think about God, or church: Christmas Eve services, carol services, perhaps Handel's *Messiah*.

Unfortunately, our world is the kind of place where we cannot expect every moment to be pure bliss. I say 'unfortunately,' but actually I suspect that bliss would not be bliss if it were unending, at least not to us now within our present still sinful state, and in our present mortal capacities. In heaven we could cope with unending bliss, but right now I think even the holiest among us are insufficiently spiritually advanced to have the capacity for that kind of sheer, constant joy. Bliss, here and now, for most of us to a large degree, and to all of us to some degree, simply necessitates 'un-bliss.' You cannot know the sheer brightness of light if there is not shadow; day is understood by contrast to night; and pleasures are sweeter when compared to pain. Expecting the more basic, perfectly good, pleasures of Christmas to last every day is like expecting to eat ice cream at every meal; you could do it but after a while it would no longer be ice cream to you, no longer be pleasant. It would become a curse, not a blessing. The old saying 'you can have too much of a good thing' is truer than we suspect. It is not trying to limit our pleasures, but heighten them. To have a mountaintop experience you have to have a valley. There are no mountains without valleys.

So I do not think—certainly not in this world—that it is truly possible (or desirable) to have Christmas every day in the two ways described above, either as perpetual commercialization or even as perpetual pleasure. Perpetual pleasure in this world is not pleasure; it is dull and ruins the possibility of pleasure. It may be that part of the point of the process of this world is to fit us to be ready to experience unending pleasures at His right hand forever. Our capacities need to be expanded to be able to contain such light. We cannot do it now.

However, there is one way in which we can experience Christmas every day. In this regard I have some sympathy with the English Puritans who tried to ban Christmas during Oliver Cromwell's reign in seventeenth century England. Doing away with 'figgy pudding' was certainly not a shrewd marketing move at the time (like banning ice cream and expecting to be popular), but behind the crassness there was a wise instinct. Christmas is not just a day. It is a life.

The life of Christmas is to live with Christ at the center of our lives. This does not mean perpetually giving ourselves, or others, gifts and presents. Nor does it mean constantly eating too much, or never working anymore and staying on permanent holiday. It means having the center of Christmas—the Christ—born in our hearts by faith so that the true meaning of Christmas can take up residence inside, in our affections, desires, will and attitude. This then shapes everything about us, who we are and what we want. It makes us live, not like Christmas, but like a Christian.

And that center of joy continues to grow and expand, despite the pain of daily existence, so that one day all that is left is to feast with the Christ we worship with our lives. Not just every day but forever and a day.

In that sense how can we have Christmas every day?

First, seek to develop the 'spirit' of Christmas. What is the true 'spirit' of Christmas? For that, look to Paul's teaching in Philippians chapter 2. There he encourages the Philippian Christians to have the spirit in them that was in Christ Jesus. What does he mean by that? He means 'being one in spirit and purpose' so to 'do nothing out of selfish ambition' that 'you should not look only to your own interests, but also to the interests of others.' In short, he says 'your attitude should be the same as that of Christ Jesus.' What does he mean by that? What does it really mean to have the same attitude as that of Christ Jesus? In Paul's famous description of the incarnation, crucifixion and glorification of Christ, he describes the extraordinary humility of Christ. He 'being in very nature God, did not consider equality with God something to be used to his own advantage.' That's the attitude we are to have! That's what it means to have the spirit of Christmas. To be people who have the attitude of Christ! We don't seek to get what we want; we seek to give ourselves for the good of others. So, in other words, to have the spirit of Christmas in us would be for our lives to be lived as redemptive tools in God's hands to rescue people in this world! What could you do to orientate your life more around the saving purpose of God? How can you grow so that what you do, the way you spend your time, is all for the grand purpose of Christ's glorification? In what way could you adjust your schedule so that you prioritize the saving of many people—even at your own personal cost, surrendering your 'dignity' so that you can serve others with the gospel? It means unity with other Christians, humility before other Christians, and a self-sacrificial mission to rescue other people to bring them to Christ.

Second, seek to develop the activity of Christmas. I don't mean the frantic mad rush for presents, or the endless round of not-too-good office parties. I mean the essential act of Christ at Christmas—the self-giving, and others-serving. Not just an attitude but an action. Who is there whom you could serve with the gospel this week? What is there that you could do to give of yourself to another person for the sake of Christ this week? How could you orientate your life around practical actions that are self-giving, loving and God-honoring? Make it practical, actual, an action. Let us not just love in words, but also deeds and in truth. To do something and say something. Is there a shut-in that you could visit? Is there someone who has less than you to whom you could give a special gift? Is there a ministry that you could support over and beyond generosity, to be generous at the crazy-generous level that Christ displayed by giving Himself in the incarnation? The truth is that many of us these days are surrounded by advice that runs counter to both the attitude and the action of the Christmas message. We are told to follow our dreams, to tell our story, to do what it takes to make progress towards our goals. Depending on how you interpret these statements—if someone is surrendered to Christ then their goals are God's goals!—then such ideas can either be fine, or quite seditious. They can be just an expression of our natural rebellious state, to build a Tower of Babel of our own dreams, and do what we can to make a name for ourselves! And we are surrounded by this sort of conversation: the celebrity or star that we are told that we can be if we try hard enough. So we need to have minds (our attitudes) and then our actions reworked by the real meaning of Christmas. In this regard then, our dreams become His dreams, and our actions become reflective of that agenda and priority. The strange thing is that *as we do this,* then we experience the joy of Christmas! If Christmas teaches us anything it is that the action of self-giving for the cause of the gospel is—at the same time—both the most sacrificial thing to do and the most joyful thing to do.

Third, seek to tell the story of Christmas. Even today, the Christmas season provides significant opportunity for the Christmas story to be told. People are more likely to go to church at Christmas than at any other time of the year, except perhaps Easter. There is an opening to think about what the story of Christmas really is, what it might mean. Part then of having Christmas every day is developing in the rhythms of our lives an opening to and opportunities for telling people about the story not just of Christmas but of Christ. What stops us from doing this? For some of us it is sheer busyness. We are so busy that we barely have time to talk to our children or our spouses, let alone talk to someone outside of the family about Jesus. Perhaps we need to take stock of our lives and see where we can build in some margin—margin for telling other people about Jesus. Perhaps you could call it 'gospel margin'! Not that the gospel should ever be in the margin, but at least try to build in some regular time to pray about and make time for someone who is not yet a Christian.

For some of us the challenge is busyness; for others of us the challenge is not so much busyness as fear. We dare not open our mouths. Why are we scared? In the end, I find this has less to do with archetypal lack of fear of God than a feeling of being ill-equipped, not knowing what to say or how to say it. The best solution to this is training. We can put on seminars, or attend seminars, that can help us with telling other people about Christ. These can be of great assistance. Sometimes the best way, though, is to find someone you know who seems to find it easy to tell other people about Jesus, and ask them how they go about doing it. Learn from them. Ask them what they do. The three great rules of telling the story of Christ are: to pray for opportunities, pray for those who preach the gospel, and make the most of the opportunities when they come along to bring people to hear the gospel preached. Be a part of the gospel of Christ being told—not just at Christmas, but throughout the year.

A story

Emma was just glad it was over. Every year she had to run around like a headless chicken, desperately trying to make sure that everything that had to happen at the Christmas season got done. It started with buying the presents. She needed to start doing that early enough so she had options to get the best possible deals. She stored the presents in a corner of their spare room, and those presents piled on top of each other until she was pretty sure she had everything she needed. Then she had to wrap them all. Emma liked to do it right, so she not only wrapped all the main presents but also the presents that went into the stockings as well. That took hours and hours. Emma actually quite enjoyed wrapping presents. She could watch Netflix while she did it. But wow did it take a long time! And then—with all that done—she felt like she had only half begun the crazy business of the season. On top of all that, the house had to be decorated. Her husband did most of that, but he had to be reminded and 'encouraged' to do it on time. And she had to make sure she enough food in the fridge ready for all the meals and special deserts that her family would expect at Christmas. Then there were all the school and children's events. There was a Christmas party for the football team, then a Christmas part for the church children's choir, then a Christmas party for the athletics team, then a Christmas party for the staff office workers and on and on and on. Frankly, it was exhausting. When Christmas itself arrived, it was all she could do to keep her temper—there seemed no moment to actually enjoy anything.

Something seemed to be missing, she knew. How could she bring the real beauty and peace (yes, peace) of the original Christmas more into her life and the life of her family? What would it look like for that message of peace and joy to envelope her life not just at Christmas but throughout the rest of the year as well? Next year, she determined, she would do two things. First, she would simplify the actual Christmas experience. One less present. One less Christmas party. One less meal. At least she would simplify a little that way. And, second, she would write down in her journal two lessons that she wanted to introduce into her life the rest of the year. That way Christmas could be just not a brief (crazily busy) season, but a message that impacted how she lived the rest of the year too.

Questions for discussion

1. Is your Christmas experience so busy you have barely any time to really think about the meaning of all the festivities?

2. What could you do to simplify your Christmas experience?

3. What two key lessons is God teaching you this Christmas?

4. Would you write those two lessons down somewhere and review them once a week for the rest of the year?

5. How could you embrace the meaning of Christmas in July?

QUESTION 8

Is Christmas Any Different From Other Holiday Programs?

When I was growing up, even in so called secular schools it was normal and expected that around Christmas you would sing a few carols and pay lip service to the traditions. Nowadays, that is not the case in any shape or form. I was first alerted to this sea change of practice when I went to a 'holiday program' for my son at his then school and became increasingly bemused by the lineup.

First of all, the 'Christian' song was 'Jingle Bells.' Now that tune is all very well (actually, I am not sure it is all very well but I am trying to be kind here) in its own place, but to call it a 'Christian' song is ridiculous. It has nothing Christian about it. To put it bluntly, it does not talk about Christ. The closest aspect of anything distinctly Christian about it is that it describes a fantasized winter scene. Such winter scenes are taken from the predominantly European memories of the weather around Christmas.

That's it. Otherwise, it is about sleighs and reindeer. It has absolutely nothing to do with Christmas at all. It is not a 'Christian' Christmas carol. It is certainly 'seasonal' and 'sweet,' but that, I am afraid, is not the same thing. If you want to sing a 'Christian' Christmas carol, then at least have the good sense to do so. Sing 'Away in a Manger' or 'Once in Royal David's City.' I don't know whether the poetry of either of those is fantastic, and there are probably theologians who can pick holes in them too, but at least they are 'Christian.'

That was my first surprise—the 'Christian' Christmas carol was 'Jingle Bells.' *You must be kidding*, I thought to myself. But then I was comforted with the idea that perhaps every other holiday would have similarly bowdlerized versions of their songs, and perhaps then that was all right. Nothing of the sort. Before too long we were singing a full-on version of some song promoting 'Kwanzaa.'

Now, this is not a partisan point, but the number of people in the world who follow Kwanzaa is small compared to the adherents of the Christ King born in Bethlehem. If you give lip service to Christians with 'Jingle Bells' (and I am not sure it is even lip service; call it fake service), then you really shouldn't serve up a full rendition of another song for any holiday celebrated by so few, comparatively speaking.

The point of this story is that there is no such thing as an ideological blank slate. If you have a 'holiday' program, you will have to make ideological decisions. Nature abhors a vacuum, and a holiday program with songs has to have songs about something—it will sing about country, or nature, or Kwanzaa, or even 'Jingle Bells,' but it will sing about something. We humans are built to worship, and worship we will. The only question is what or whom. Even the word 'holiday' gives the game away: it is a 'holy day,' the word coming from the holy days that the church set up eons ago. You cannot escape making ultimate decisions on your take on public holidays, especially at holiday programs.

What makes Christmas any different from all this? Much in every way, but, to begin with, Christmas is straightforward and transparent. It is the worship of the Christ, the feast of celebration of the Christ. You may not agree with that, but at least you know where you stand. No George Orwellian doublespeak there.

Certainly, there have been other religions (pagan ones) that talked about a 'god' coming down and siring a child with a maiden, but that is not the Christmas story. So unique is the Christmas story that it took the church several hundred years before it could come up with a form of language to express it. Jesus is 'fully God and fully man', 'one Person, two natures'. That it is not really saying any more than that you shall call Him 'Emmanuel', meaning 'God with us', but the idea, the concept, the reality, the event, was so unique that we even had to develop a new form of talking to describe it.

Christmas is not just a holiday program. It is the Christ-event. And that is far more than 'Jingle Bells.'

How do we emphasize Christmas' distinctiveness, its unique aspects, and all that it is truly meant to be celebrating and proclaiming?

First, distinguish the history from the tradition. Certainly, Christmas occurs at the time of the year where there have been—and still are—other mid-winter festivals of one kind or another. You can make a case even for Christmas trees having origins in some sort of murky pagan past in the depths of Europe. But that is not to say that Christmas itself is damned by such an association. After all, while there is something natural about wanting to eat good food and have some sort of festival of lights during the dark months of Christmas, that we celebrate this occurrence through the Christmas message suggests that we are saying something different and distinctive. It is natural to want to celebrate birthdays; when we celebrate our own birthday we are saying something distinctive and unique about who we are, because it is our own particular birthday. Humans like to celebrate. Why? What is meant to be the focal point of that celebration? The Christmas (and the Christian) claim is that the focal point of that celebration is the historical birth, life, death and resurrection of Jesus Christ. Traditions grow up around Christmas. Many of us enjoy them. But the fact that such traditions have been used at other times and in other places to celebrate other ideas does not mean that the event we use to celebrate Christ is thereby consigned to the same guilt by association. A car can be used as a weapon, or as an ambulance to rescue someone. A Christmas tree can be used to celebrate Christ, even if that tree has some sort of pagan origins to it. It is important therefore to focus on the meaning of Christmas, the history of it, and not get distracted by the claim that certain traditions and celebrations are used in other winter celebrations.

Second, emphasize the person not the activity. There is a lot of activity around Christmas—carol services, Christmas parties, etc. etc. All well and good; there is nothing wrong with enjoying a good sing-song, or a good party with friends. But if we *only* focus on these activities it can perhaps seem as if we are just doing the same as everyone else, or any other kind of celebration. What is different between this, we might think, and another religious celebration, or even just hanging with family in the middle of winter for no other reason than that we like being with our family? So we need to emphasize not just the celebratory activity, but the person around whom such activity is meant to center. Think of Him. Think of what He did. Read Scripture passages about Him. Talk about Him. When you open a present think of the gift of Christ for you. When you give a present think of the gift of Christ for the world. When you sing songs, think of the meaning of those songs and not just the pleasure that comes from the tune that you remember as a child. If we don't emphasize the person (and not just the activity) it could become a bit like going to a birthday party where everyone has fun but the person whose birthday it is is forgotten! Everyone is having a good time, but we have forgotten the real reason why we are there. The birthday celebrations carry on, but the birthday itself is not remembered. The trouble with that is partly that before too long the lack of reason for the celebration will become apparent—and people will stop bothering to come to such a pointless celebration. It is also that the person whom we are meant to be celebrating is forgotten. That is rude and unkind, when it is about another human being whose birthday we are meant to be remembering. But it is much more than merely rude or impolite when we celebrate Christmas but do it only focusing on the activity and not the person we are meant to be celebrating. That person is Christ! The Son of God! Focus there! Honor Him! Worship Him!

Third, look forward and not just back. Christmas, you see, is not only about the baby who came. The whole focus of Christmas, and especially Advent that leads up to Christmas, is also future orientated. We are looking forward to the day when Christ returns. And as such, the celebration of Christmas is saved from mere nostalgia, and becomes something more powerful. More fearful. More joyful. It is something that can speak with greater integrity to the 'hopes and fears of all the years', because not only are they 'met' in Jesus who was born in the manger, they are also finally fulfilled in His coming return. Without that future focus we can lose a sense of credibility about the claims of Christmas. Has Jesus really brought peace on earth? Yes, in the intended sense of the angels who sang about that peace on earth—peace in the reconciliation of God with man through faith in Jesus and the grace that is given to those that whom God calls. Yes, there is peace. And there is growing peace—wholeness, integration, *shalom*—as we increasingly give our lives to Jesus and follow Him with complete commitment.

But still that peace is not yet finalized. We must look forward, Christmas is telling us. Just like the Old Testament believers had to wait for the redemption that came in Jesus, so we are waiting. We are waiting for that day when He will return. Not now as a baby born in a manger. But as the Lord of all glory, power and might, to gather to Himself all those who are His. There is a great day of judgment coming when He separates the sheep from the goats. We better get right with Him now, Christmas is also saying. He is coming. Sooner than we expect. At a time that we do not expect. Make the most of this opportunity, this Christmas, then, not just to look back (with a sort of religious sentimentality), but also to look forward. To realize that one day all the wrongs of this world will be righted. To look forward with joy, that one day you will see Him and be with Him and be where He is and He will take you to a place that He has prepared for you. To look forward with hope—not the uncertain wishing of 'I hope so', but the confident biblical hope that is grounded in God's promises, and the gift of Jesus at Christmas, that gives us a future hope that is firm and secure, an anchor for our souls. Even in the midst of all the storms and uncertainties of our lives. Christmas not only means He came, but that He is coming back!

A story

Brett went to the school Christmas (or was it now 'holiday'?) program without any great expectations of anything dramatic happening. Someone stood up and gave a fair rendition of 'All I Want for Christmas Is You.' The person singing didn't have Mariah Carey's vocal cords, but then again who does? Everyone applauded after the solo. It was still pretty good—and impressive to be able to pull off that song with even anything like a passing impression of Mariah Carey's version. Then (of course) someone else did a version of 'White Christmas.' Nothing could match Bing Crosby's single—after all that is the world's best selling single of all time with sales around 50 million or so—but again it wasn't too bad. And once more everyone applauded. Now the mood was really Christmassy. Most people seemed to be in a really happy frame of mind, and there was a lot of goodwill around as people beamed at each merrily—Brett wondered whether a few of the parents hadn't come to the school program a bit merry in more ways than one.

But then something did happen. First of all, there was 'Jingle Bells.' Of course, Brett thought, there's bound to be Jingle Bells. Personally, he didn't have anything against the song—in fact he quite liked it. The song was the ultimate in Christmas sentimentality. But still, if you had to do the schmaltzy Christmas sentimentality then Jingle Bells was definitely the way to go. Next, though, there was a surprise. A small, young, pre-pubescent teenage boy got up to the microphone and begun to sing. Now he had a voice—wow. And what he sung was 'Once in Royal David's City.'

> *He came down to earth from heaven,*
> *Who is God and Lord of all,*
> *And His shelter was a stable,*
> *And His cradle was a stall;*
> *With the poor and meek and lowly,*
> *Lived on earth our Savior holy.*

The performance was extraordinary—such a pure and yet powerful voice. And Brett began to think about more than the performance, he started to think about the meaning. Could it be that this baby was 'God and Lord of all'? That really would be something to sing about.

Questions for discussion

1. What was your favorite Christmas or holiday program?

2. What made it different from any of the others that you have been to?

3. Do you have a favorite Christmas carol? Could you learn a stanza of that carol to encourage and motivate you in your following of Jesus?

4. What is unique about Christmas?

5. How could the distinctive elements of Christmas impact how you plan your holidays during the Christmas period?

QUESTION 9

Did It Really Happen?

So did it? Was there really a star that 'hung' over Bethlehem? Were there actually three wise men coming from afar? What about the shepherds watching their flocks by night? How much of this is real and how much is tradition, fantasy, or (ever-so-nice) make believe?

Let's start with a few shockers. Nowhere in the Bible does it say there were three wise men. It tells us that they brought gifts of gold, frankincense and myrrh (three gifts)—and from that has grown up the tradition that there were three wise men. In theory, there could have been ten or twenty or two. We just do not know.

The issue of the star is a little trickier to unpack. Theories as to how to interpret the biblical data are many. It is certainly possible to read the biblical account to mean that there was a supernatural event with a star moving from one place to another. Given that believing the Christmas story means believing that the Son of God was born of a virgin, there seems no difficulty with accepting that the star could have simply been a supernatural phenomenon. If you can accept the one, you should be able to accept the other (less massive) miracle. But the biblical account does not, most think, necessarily mean the star itself had to be a supernatural event, though it was an event ordered by God and planned by Him. Some have said it was a shooting star or a comet; others have said it was a particular constellation that was associated with kingship in Israel. At any rate, one way or another, the magi from the East did travel and find the one born King of the Jews.

The bigger issue with this story, of course, is not the peripheral details and miracles, but the great big whacking monster of a miracle in the center of them all: Jesus born of a virgin. The Son of God—fully God and fully man in one person—entered the world to save us. Some people think that science makes that explanation of the event impossible, and they say that people only accepted it when they were pre-scientific. But people have known where babies came from for a long time, and in fact the biblical account tells us that Joseph thought that the natural explanation for Mary's pregnancy was the only possible one—until an angel told him otherwise.

It really comes back to our explanatory grid, our framework. If we think that God exists, then it is perfectly possible for God to have been born as a man. This is not beyond possibility, for God, by definition, can do whatever He likes. This does not mean that Christians believe that miracles happen all the time; if they did, they would not be miracles. God is a God of order, and the scientific practice was begun out of an assumption that because God was ordered, so His world would have order too: 'thinking God's thoughts after him' (Kepler). But while miracles are rare (they are rare even in the Bible), God as God is perfectly able to do them.

The question is not *could it have happened?* (yes) but *did it happen?* If you accept the biblical witness, you will accept that it did happen. For those who are not sure whether they can follow what the Bible says yet, the Bible points in a different direction for evidence to guarantee its message. Not to the incarnation (Jesus' birth) but to the resurrection. That is the place, witnessed by many, where we have evidence that God was in Christ reconciling the world to Himself. This Jesus, fully God and fully man in one person, died and rose again. His word is sure. He commissioned His apostles and disciples to write the New Testament. We have a certain word therefore about the incarnation.

It really happened. Here are some ways that you can argue with yourself (or others) to establish the historical veracity of the incarnation:

First, be practical. If Jesus were not born the Son of God, then what else can explain the data? Certainly, there were many other religious stories from around ancient times. But which of them is still in existence, and still massively growing throughout the world—and is indeed by far the largest religion in the world? Answer: none of them. So what explains the data of the extraordinary impact of Christianity, if it is not the practical factuality of the incarnation, death and resurrection of the Son of God? Various options have been suggested over the years. Most commonly, that there was a unique combination of movements and desires at that time in history that meant that the situation was simply ripe for a movement like Christianity. The trouble with that is that there were other movements a bit like Christianity—mystery religions from the East, for instance—that gained no real long term traction. There was something distinct, even unique, about Christianity that gave it a certain long-term sticking power and a massive historical global impact. This is a very practical argument (what else can account for the data?) but it is an important one. Sometimes Christians are accused of being eminently unrealistic and impractical. It's all head-in-the-clouds, pie-in-the-sky, nonsense. But put your mind back in time, and ask yourself what else can account for the practical data.

2 Second, be historical. The data we are talking about so far is historical. But you might say it is all confined to the books that were written by Christians. Surely this is the very definition of bias? It's like looking for objective data about your favorite sports team from the writings of their fan club! But there are two ways this line of thinking, that dismisses the historical evidence, can be seen not to be persuasive. One line of thinking follows the actual way the evidence is presented in the biblical accounts. If this were 'fan fiction', then you would expect certain ways of writing. In particular, you would expect all the difficulties to be ironed out. And you would certainly expect that the early church leaders would come across as hero figures. Instead, they are frequently presented as imbeciles, or at least slow on the uptake, and even at times spiritual and morally questionable. This is no fan fiction. At times it's almost confessional, raw, authentically vulnerable and honest. The other line of thinking which helps with this objection, that all the historical data comes from writings by Christians, is just the plain fact that it isn't true. You will find, albeit brief, significant references—and by no means always flattering—to the early Christian movement in ancient historical writers like Suetonius, Josephus and Tacitus. These references do not go into great detail, and are not lengthy; but this is exactly what you would expect regarding a movement that, at the time, was regarded with great suspicion and was very early in its influence and still hugely marginalized by the powers that be.

Third, be philosophical. 'Philosophy' (and its easier-sounding partner 'worldviews') is generally regarded with a healthy suspicion as being all theory and no use to the practical man or woman. But we all have a philosophy of life, or a worldview, whether we are aware of it or not. What do we think happens after we die? What do we think is the purpose of life? What do we think is the best way to handle suffering? Why is there suffering? All these questions and many answers are the bread and butter of philosophical thinking—and cognizant or not we all have a way of looking at life that attempts either to answer them, or, for some, avoid answering them! Now, when it comes to the incarnation (Jesus being born the Son of God), a lot of people's objections come down to philosophical objections. This, they think, is just not the sort of thing that happens. The reason why they think like that is either because they don't think God exists at all, or they think that if He does exist there is no way He could/would break the laws of nature and make such an event occur. So we begin to look at the data—practical, historical—from a philosophical point of view. There's no real way to avoid this. We all have frameworks through which we interpret data. It's impossible to live without adopting some sort of set of frameworks. But the point is to be aware of those frameworks—and then adjust them if the data so suggests that we should. Such a paradigm shift (as Thomas Kuhn famously called it) is always painful, at least for those who are personally invested in the older paradigm. We sense a feeling of loss, and of disorientation about how the new framework is going to operate. We can resist the date (practical, historical) in order to avoid the negative feelings that can come as we transition to a new, and better, way of looking at life. I understand all that: I've made some paradigm shifts in my life, and it does take time to get your mind around it, and your heart engaged with it. But as we look at the data around the Christmas event, it is important to be aware of our biases and predispositions. And to realize that if we do not accept the Christ-event at this point, we will likely be biased against accepting it. And that our friends, if we are Christians, will likewise be biased against accepting it. We prefer what is safe and easy, over what is true. Perhaps the greatest illustration of this in modern times was the tendency of the ruling classes to ignore what was going on in Nazi Germany. If they looked carefully, the evidence was there. But the last thing anyone wanted was another war. And so, their minds consistently refused to accept the evidence as it was presented to them. Anything but that!

Fourth, be personal. There's no getting around that in the end this is a personal and relational matter. We've talked a lot about the 'data' in this chapter—emphasizing objective and factual matters to make the case that there are good reasons to accept the incarnation. But this is more than merely a rational matter. Becoming a Christian is more like falling in love than buying a car. Or, to put it better, it's more like getting married than buying a car. When you get married there is an emotional element, of course. On the other hand, if you are wise, you would not marry someone for whom you are sure, for objective reasons and on rational grounds, that you are not a good fit. Marry in haste, repent at leisure. This is why one goes out on dates; this is why you ask your friends' opinion of the person you are dating. This is why, if you are wise, and if you have good parents, you ask the opinion of your parents. This is why, again, if you are wise, you do things like premarital counseling. You're not only trying to get ready for marriage, you're testing the relationship to see whether it is a good fit. So there is much that is rational about it. There is real data involved: do we get along together in various situations? Do we have similar values and goals and dreams? Do we want the same things? Are we compatible in terms of personality? But while there are these elements that we can test over time and in conversation with others, there are also more subjective parts to it. And at the end of day, when you walk down the aisle with someone, you are making a commitment that is based on a promise, not based upon certainty. You are vowing in sickness and in health, because the future might mean sickness and it might mean health—and no one, but God, knows for sure. Similarly, to some extent, with your commitment to Christ. It is a covenant vow. And there are factual and objective data. But at the end of the data it is a walk of faith, a step of faith, a personal trust—a commitment of your whole self to this other person. And there are some things that you just can't find out until you do get married, until you do commit yourself to Christ for the first time or again this Christmas.

A story

Sarah had always liked the Christmas story. But she had also always assumed that it was just a myth—a made-up story, fictional, albeit one with the respect that comes from having been around for such a very long time. There were many parts of the story that seemed to Sarah to be obviously mythical. To begin with, the whole idea of a virgin birth seemed obviously not only ridiculous, but also the sort of idea that resonated with other ancient myths from pagan times. She was amused when that Stars Wars prequel talked about a 'vergence in the force'—that was, for Sarah, another example of the way that humans have this mythical desire for some mystical power in a newborn baby. But it wasn't history, of course not.

But then while she was at College, Sarah came across some students who actually believed that the whole thing happened. When she said to them that surely the parents of Jesus were just ignorant peasants, their reply that even in those days the people knew where babies came from somewhat unnerved her. It appeared as if her friends at College had really thought through the factuality of the incarnation a lot more than she had assumed. She started to do some research, and she realized there were significant differences between the ancient myths and the Christmas story. Christians did not, for instance, believe that 'God had sex with Mary'; they believed there was a God-becoming-man event. A lot of that was beyond Sarah's mind to comprehend, but that didn't surprise her. After all, if this was God then she would expect there were parts of what she was researching that would point to an essence that was above human comprehension. What was more troubling to Sarah, as she looked into it, was that the texts all indicated that it took people a long time to accept that Jesus was really who claimed to be. That had the ring of truth to it, Sarah thought. And it was impressive that the early witnesses recorded their (and others) initial hesitating in believing that Jesus was born God. It added to that weighty feeling that Sarah maybe was coming across The Real Thing. And then when she read C. S. Lewis' description that Christianity was 'the true myth', Sarah started to find herself—almost against her own feelings but in line with her reasoning—believing.

Questions for discussion

1. Do you think the incarnation is a credible event for contemporary people to believe?

2. What do you think is the most intellectually satisfying and persuasive part of the incarnation story?

3. Do you think it is reasonable to expect that if we met the real story about the real God, we would find elements that would be beyond our comprehension (not against our apprehension)?

4. The Bible teaches that every part of us, including our minds, is tainted by the effects of the fall. Is it surprising then that we sometimes find it hard to believe the truth about God?

5. How can we increasingly have the mind of Christ, and love God not just with our feelings but also with our minds?

Should I Go To Church At Christmas?

Yes! Let me give a slightly fuller answer. It starts with understanding the nature of the 'church.' First what church is *not*. Church is *not* a bunch of people coming together to sing old-fashioned songs that no one has ever heard of before. Church is *not* a building. Church is *not* a certain religious tradition which emphasizes doing the right thing and being moral. Church is *not* a religious club. Church is *not* an institution or organization. Church is *not* a franchise of a religious business.

So what is church? Church is the body of Christ. That's it. The church is Christ's extension of His body here on earth. The church has a mission, therefore, and that mission is the extension of Christ's mission. Our mission is to make known the gospel to the ends of the earth. Starting locally, going globally. Our mission is to follow Christ, that is, to do what Christ would do as His body here on earth.

That means it's not really a matter of 'going to church.' The question 'Should I go to church?' assumes a certain understanding of what a church *is*. It assumes that a church is located primarily (if not exclusively) in a certain place: you go *to* church. It assumes that a church is primarily (if not exclusively) a meeting that you attend probably once a week: you *go* to church. It assumes that a church is a voluntary event which you can decide for yourself whether to attend: you go to *church*. It assumes that, finally, it is your decision about your involvement that matters: *you* go to church.

Most of all it assumes that to do so would be unpleasant, boring, and (especially) dutiful: you *should* go to church.

What if none of that is the case?

What if instead church is the body of Christ? That means, number one, to be a part of it you first of all have to have a personal, deep, spiritual connection with Christ. You have to know Christ. You have to believe in Christ (not just that He existed, but trust Him personally). You have to be 'in' Christ. You have to have the Spirit of Christ in you. And then that means, number two, that you now follow Christ by aiming to do, by the power of His Spirit that dwells within you, what He would do and what He asks you to do in His Word, the Bible.

So should you go to church at Christmas? Absolutely, yes. When you go, you will have the opportunity (at a biblical church) to meet the real Jesus Christ of the Bible. You will have the opportunity to come across other followers of Jesus. You will have the opportunity to be a part of the agency in the world—the body of Christ—which has the greatest mission in the world, and the greatest responsibility: to make disciples of all nations for the glory of God.

CHURCH: *CH*ristians *U R* the body of *CH*rist. Don't just go to church, be the church, live the church, act the church. Every day, every week, every year. Like Christ.

How? There are many descriptions in the Bible of what the church is meant to be. In what way does Christmas itself, though, help us shape the way a church should function and be—and how does that impact your own particular role or commitment to the local church?

First, worship. The New Testament church in Acts 2 gathered together regularly. They came together in the temple courts each day to worship! There is a great tendency for Christians in the West to look at church attendance as something that is optional—or, if necessary, at least infrequent. But look at the New Testament church! How they loved to gather together! What has happened to us? How is it that we have lost our first love? Let us be the kind of Christians who—like the wise men—will not just meander into church if we happen to get up on time that particular Sunday, but even journey great distances to come to worship Christ. I know, we often think of church as an 'institution' and so we are wary about committing to an institution. We don't like the idea of the potential power dynamics at work—we wonder who is footing the bills. Is there some sort of deep multi-level marketing going on, are they after our money? Who here is really in charge and what do they want from me? But maybe that's not the dynamic at all. Maybe it is—as the Bible says that it is!—the body of Christ. Maybe it is an organization, but not just an organization; maybe it's also an organism! What a great joy, then, to gather for worship with the body of Christ; the bride of Christ; the temple of God's people; the house of God; that we, like living stones, are being built up together. Think of those shepherds traveling in joy to go and see whether those things are true. Go to church like that!

Second, outreach. Perhaps no greater sign of being in love is the desire to tell other people about what you are experiencing. We sing about it. We write poems about it. We want to speak about it. And when we are in love with Christ and His people we will want to tell other people about Christ and our church. This also happened on that first Christmas. The shepherds went back to their fields praising God for all they had seen. Can you imagine shouting through the neighborhood, waking people up, singing hallelujah! That would make quite a change from how we sometimes come back from a late night Christmas Eve service! YES! Praise God! But whether in loud, or quieter ways, we get out and we tell others about God, we tell others about the story of Christmas, we tell others what we have seen and heard. This is such a key part of being the body of Christ: the mission of Christ. We are not simply 'going to church'; we are being salt and light. We are on a mission. We are thinking about the needs of those around us. We are thinking about how we can reach this city for Christ's glory. We are representing the King who was born Savior of the world—not a religious social club, but a band of brothers and sisters on a mission to rescue the dying! Rescue them! Let outreach be your watchword this Christmas! How can you bring people to Christ? How can you bring people to your gospel-preaching church? Don't just go to church; bring others along with you. It's amazing how open people are to being invited if we love them and like them and smile at them and invite them. Try it and see—see how many people you can bring to church this Christmas! Next year see if you can beat your record! Make it a competition among your friends—in a friendly way—I've invited five people, how about that! Let's get creative with parties, and get togethers, and all sorts of ways to get the Word out and get the people in to see the one who was born King, the Savior of the world!

Third, relationships. Loving relationships are such an important part of church. See that holy family, gathered. Joseph and Mary and the Baby Jesus. Let us put aside our wrangling and arguing. Our petty squabbling and fighting. Let us not quarrel over meaningless words. Let us not hold grudges. Let us seek forgiveness and seek to forgive. Let us be slow to anger and abounding in mercy. How the world watches how Christians relate, and how people long to find a community where they can truly find joy and peace and—yes—love in community together. Are there people that you are alienated from in your church? What could you do this Christmas to reconcile with them? Could you give them a gift? Could you give them a gift of 'I'm sorry, please forgive me'? It takes great humility to ask for forgiveness. But that is often the first step to a higher and greater university. If it is true, as the pagan saying is, that they whom the gods wish to destroy they first make insane in their practices and foolish decisions, it is certainly true that humility is the royal road to effectiveness in God's kingdom. Humble yourself under God's mighty hand that in due course He might lift you up. So much of this is the expression of Christmas: forgiveness of sins, the humility of Christ, the loving family of that first New Testament Church gathered around the manger in worship of Jesus. Come and join in, bow the knee before Him, and bend your heart to be merciful and forgiving to your brother or sister who bows next to you. Be reconciled to God and reconciled to each other in Christ!

Fourth, discipleship. Churches are places of training too. How can we grow into the likeness of Christ? How can we become more like Christ? What sins do we need to repent of and discipline ourselves to avoid? What character traits can we ask God to give us more of? What courses in Bible study could we join to grow more like Christ? The story of Christmas is much about this. Mary heard all these things and treasured them in her heart. She did not understand everything yet but she wanted to figure it out and grow in her understanding. She was not just the Mother of Christ; she was the first of the disciples of Christ, and she had much to learn and grow in. What can you learn this Christmas? What book could you read? What Bible passage could you learn and memorize? Could you take the time this Christmas to join a small group, or adult Sunday school class? Could you take the time this Christmas to pray that God would find someone to disciple you personally? Could you take the time to disciple someone yourself—and if you're not sure how to do that ask someone who is older than you in the Christian faith to show you how? We are meant to be disciples making disciples, not consumers consuming food. How could we become more like Christ in making disciples and being a disciple this Christmas?

A story

Amy felt that church was for other people. One time she was reading a blog that argued that the day of the institutional church was over. Amy resonated with that approach. She wanted Jesus. She wanted nothing to do with church. Amy knew that some of it was personal. Nothing really bad had happened to her in the church. But when she was growing up she had increasingly come across the reality of church—and over time it had turned her off. She'd heard the old joke 'if you find a perfect church don't join it, you'll only spoil it.' She knew that church was a hospital for sinners, not a museum for saints. She was not expecting perfection from the church. The trouble for Amy was that much of her church experience seemed so different from her reading of what the church was in the New Testament. Of course, the church in New Testament times had lots of problems too. It wasn't the problems that she saw in contemporary churches that concerned Amy. It was that the church seemed a different thing—a different entity, not the same as what she read about in the New Testament church. She walked into church in her city and while everyone seemed nice enough, the actual experience of church was so prosaic, manufactured, unreal, that it left her thinking she'd wished she'd stayed home and read her Bible by herself.

But Christmas came around again and so Amy went off to church once more. She hadn't been to church since Easter. There she was again, at church, not expecting to get much out of it, but feeling as if at least a couple of times a year she should go to church with everyone else. Frankly, Amy felt very out of place. She found the whole experience grating. The time when everyone stood up and greeted each other was awkward to say the least. Amy was not an introvert, she liked people. But she wasn't at church to meet other people. She went to the pub for that. She was at church to meet with God. Where was He? Would He show up? She knew that was a sort of ridiculous way to think— God was omnipresent after all. But wasn't the church meant to be the body of Christ? Shouldn't we expect to encounter God in some special way when the church gathered?

And then it happened. Gradually, as Amy was thinking along these lines she became aware that the person being spoken to through the sermon was herself. It seemed as if the sermon had been written for her. The concerns and questions she had were being tackled one by one. It was almost as if God had told the preacher what to say because God already knew that Amy was going *to be there that day. The fact that Amy hadn't finally decided to go to church until about 10 minutes before the service began sort of freaked out Amy. Obviously, God knew before Amy herself knew that Amy was going to be in church that week—He'd been preparing the preacher all week to address Amy's questions. And as her questions were addressed and answered she began to realize that her issues with the contemporary question were not that it was so different from the New Testament church, but that it was so like the New Testament church. So similar—in all its strengths and weaknesses—and she had been running not from church but from God. Amy began to quietly cry as she realized anew how much God loved her, wanted her, and was pursuing her to bring her to Himself.*

Questions for discussion

1. How many churches do you have that exist within a twenty-mile radius of where you live? (You can find out by doing a Google search for 'churches near me').

2. Do you know what you need to look for to find a biblical church? Here's a website with a search engine that can help you at least begin to find a church that is all about the gospel of Jesus Christ: https://www.thegospelcoalition.org/churches/

3. What sort of attitude change would it take for you to think less of what you can get out of church and more what you can give to church?

4. Do you pray for your church leaders?

5. What areas of service are you involved with in your church?

Also available from Christian Focus …

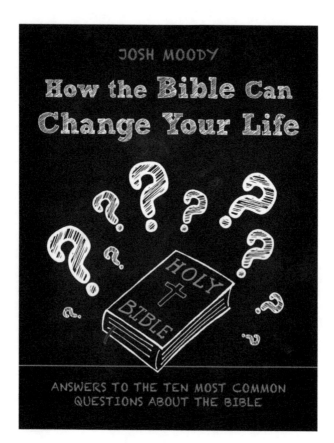

JOSH MOODY

How the Bible Can Change Your Life

ANSWERS TO THE TEN MOST COMMON
QUESTIONS ABOUT THE BIBLE

ISBN 978-1-5271-0151-7

How the Bible Can Change Your Life
Answers to the Ten Most Common Questions about the Bible
Josh Moody

Christians are Bible people. We believe that God speaks to us through His inspired Word. And yet many Christians and churches don't actually open their Bibles. Josh Moody asks the question: Why should I read the Bible?

Moody's book will greatly help a wide range of readers—the beginner, the Bible-hungry believer, the confused—and will minister particularly to the brilliant thinker who needs strong but succinct arguments dipped in supernatural realities. The great need of the modern church is confidence in and affection for the Word of God. How the Bible Can Change Your Life *is just the book for times like ours.*

Owen Strachan,
Associate Professor of Christian Theology, Midwestern Baptist
Theological Seminary, Kansas City, Missouri

A powerful blend of penetrating argument and practical application, this is a God-centred challenge to prevailing contemporary attitudes. It will send you back to the Bible with renewed confidence and fresh expectation.

David Jackman,
Past President, The Proclamation Trust, London

Christian Focus Publications

Our mission statement –

STAYING FAITHFUL

In dependence upon God we seek to impact the world through literature faithful to His infallible Word, the Bible. Our aim is to ensure that the Lord Jesus Christ is presented as the only hope to obtain forgiveness of sin, live a useful life and look forward to heaven with Him.

Our books are published in four imprints:

CHRISTIAN FOCUS

Popular works including biographies, commentaries, basic doctrine and Christian living.

CHRISTIAN HERITAGE

Books representing some of the best material from the rich heritage of the church.

MENTOR

Books written at a level suitable for Bible College and seminary students, pastors, and other serious readers. The imprint includes commentaries, doctrinal studies, examination of current issues and church history.

CF4•K

Children's books for quality Bible teaching and for all age groups: Sunday school curriculum, puzzle and activity books; personal and family devotional titles, biographies and inspirational stories – because you are never too young to know Jesus!

Christian Focus Publications Ltd,
Geanies House, Fearn, Ross-shire,
IV20 1TW, Scotland, United Kingdom.
www.christianfocus.com
blog.christianfocus.com